Henry J.L.J Massé

The Cathedral Church of Gloucester

A description of its fabric and a brief history of the Episcopal see

Henry J.L.J Massé

The Cathedral Church of Gloucester
A description of its fabric and a brief history of the Episcopal see

ISBN/EAN: 9783337260705

Printed in Europe, USA, Canada, Australia, Japan

Cover: Foto ©ninafisch / pixelio.de

More available books at **www.hansebooks.com**

BELL'S CATHEDRAL SERIES:
EDITED BY GLEESON WHITE
AND EDWARD F. STRANGE

GLOUCESTER

Photochrom Co. Ltd. [Photo.]
GLOUCESTER CATHEDRAL, FROM THE ROOF OF ST. JOHN'S CHURCH.

THE CATHEDRAL CHURCH OF
GLOUCESTER
A DESCRIPTION OF ITS FABRIC AND A BRIEF HISTORY OF THE EPISCOPAL SEE

BY H. J. L. J. MASSÉ, M.A.

WITH FORTY-NINE ILLUSTRATIONS

LONDON   GEORGE BELL & SONS   1898

W. H. WHITE AND CO. LTD.
RIVERSIDE PRESS, EDINBURGH

GENERAL PREFACE

This series of monographs has been planned to supply visitors to the great English Cathedrals with accurate and well illustrated guide-books at a popular price. The aim of each writer has been to produce a work compiled with sufficient knowledge and scholarship to be of value to the student of Archæology and History, and yet not too technical in language for the use of an ordinary visitor or tourist.

To specify all the authorities which have been made use of in each case would be difficult and tedious in this place. But amongst the general sources of information which have been almost invariably found useful are:—(1) the great county histories, the value of which, especially in questions of genealogy and local records, is generally recognised; (2) the numerous papers by experts which appear from time to time in the Transactions of the Antiquarian and Archæological Societies; (3) the important documents made accessible in the series issued by the Master of the Rolls; (4) the well-known works of Britton and Willis on the English Cathedrals; and (5) the very excellent series of Handbooks to the Cathedrals originated by the late Mr John Murray; to which the reader may in most cases be referred for fuller detail, especially in reference to the histories of the respective sees.

GLEESON WHITE,
E. F. STRANGE,
Editors of the Series.

AUTHOR'S PREFACE

I wish to express my great obligations to Mr F. S. Waller (the Cathedral Architect) for his courtesy and kindness in allowing me to make the fullest use of his "Notes and Sketches" of the Cathedral, a book which is now, unfortunately, out of print; to Mr W. H. St. John Hope, F.S.A., for permission to quote from his "Notes on the Benedictine Abbey of St. Peter at Gloucester," published in the Records of Gloucester Cathedral; also to the Records of Gloucester Cathedral.

To Mr E. J. Burrow I owe special thanks for permission to use blocks made from his black-and-white drawings, one of which has not been published before; to the Very Rev. the Dean for much useful information and assistance; and lastly to the Sub-Sacrist, Mr T. W. G. Cooke, whose help has been at all times ungrudging and invaluable.

H. J. L. J. M.

CONTENTS

	PAGE
CHAPTER I.—History of the Building	3
CHAPTER II.—The Exterior of the Cathedral :	14
The West Front	20
The South Front and Porch	20
The South Transept	21
The Tower and the Bells	22
The Lady Chapel	26
CHAPTER III.—The Interior :	28
The Nave	32
The West End and South Aisle	36
The West Windows and the Font	40
The North Aisle	41
The Choir Screen	44
The Organ	46
The Choir	47
The Reredos	56
The South Transept	65
Chapel of St. Andrew and 'Prentice Bracket	67
The Crypt	68
South Ambulatory of Choir	72
Triforium of the Choir	73
The Whispering Gallery	77
The Lady Chapel	79
Abbot Boteler's Chapel	85
The North Transept	89
CHAPTER IV.—The Precincts and Monastic Buildings :	94
The Vineyard, the Dorter, the Refectory	95
The Little Cloisters	96
The Library	98
The Chapter-House	101
The Cloisters	104
The Monks' Lavatory	108
The Slype	111
The Deanery	112
CHAPTER V.—List of Abbots and Bishops of Gloucester	117
The City	122
Other Churches and Monastic Foundations	124
Remains of Old Gloucester	128
Notes Architectural and Chronological	133

ILLUSTRATIONS

	PAGE
The Cathedral from St. John's Tower . . . *Frontispiece*	
The Tower from the East	2
Bird's-eye view of Norman Work	15
The Cathedral from the South-West	17
The Cathedral from North-West corner of the Cloisters	19
The Tower from the Palace Yard	21
View of the Cathedral in 1727	23
South Porch since the Restoration	25
Piscina in the Triforium	27
The Nave, looking East	29
The Nave and North Aisle	33
South Aisle of the Nave	37
Plan of the Original Choir Screen	44
The Choir, looking East	49
Plan of the Original High-Altar	51
Sketch of Old Norman Choir	52
The Choir, looking West	53
The Choir in 1806	57
Plan of the Triforium of the Choir	61
South-East Chapel in the Crypt	69
Plan of the Crypt	71
South-East View of Cathedral	75
Triforium of the Choir, looking East	76
South Ambulatory of the Choir	78
The Lady Chapel	81
West End of Lady Chapel	83
Tomb of Robert Curthose	87
North Ambulatory of the Choir, looking East	90
North Ambulatory of the Choir, looking West	91
Door from North Transept into North Ambulatory of the Choir	92
St. Mary's and King Edward's Gates	96
College and Palace Yard Gateways	97
Remains of Infirmary	98
Mediæval House	99
Chapter-House (Plan)	102
Plan of Abbey Precincts	103
Cloister Garth from North-West	107
The Monks' Lavatory	109
Plan of Old Tank in the Cloister Garth	111
The Cloister, showing the Carrels of the Monks	113
South Aisle of Nave	116
Monument to Mrs Morley	121
The Old Judge's House	125
The House of Robert Raikes	127
The New Inn	129
Carving at New Inn Lane	130
Remains of Roman Wall	131
Plan of Cathedral (with Dimensions)	134, 135

A

GLOUCESTER CATHEDRAL

CHAPTER I

HISTORY OF THE BUILDING

It is neither possible, nor desirable, within the limits of a book of this size and scope, to go fully into the question, interesting though it be, of the relative claims of Aldred and Serlo to the honour of the first building of the Abbey of Gloucester. Professor Willis, in his lecture addressed to the meeting of the Archæological Institute, held at Gloucester in 1860, after giving various reasons for believing that the crypt dates back no further than 1089, when the foundation-stone was laid by Abbot Serlo, goes on to state that he was "clearly of opinion that when the foundations of the cathedral were laid, the crypt was planned to receive the existing superstructure and no other."

Professor Freeman, in his lecture published in the "Records of Gloucester Cathedral," says: "The first thing we do know for certain is, that in the year 1089, thirty-one years only after the dedication of Ealdred's church, Serlo, the first Norman Abbot, began the building of a new church, which was itself dedicated in 1100."

From the record quoted by Mr W. H. Hart ("Chartulary," i. 3), the first mention of the abbey is in 681, when it was founded by Osric, viceroy of King Ethelred. It was dedicated to St. Peter, and Kyneburga (the sister of Osric) was the first Abbess of a double foundation for monks and nuns. She died in 710.

Osric himself was buried in his church in 729 (Hart, i. 5), and his sister was buried near him, in front of the altar of St. Petronilla, which was on the north side of the then existing church.

The second Abbess was also a lady of royal descent, and

widow of Wulphere, King of the Mercians. She died in 735, and with Eve or Eva, or Gaffa, her successor, who died in 769, the monastery came to an end.

In 823 a new *régime* began—viz. that of secular priests, introduced by Beornwulf, King of Mercia, and the *Monasticon Anglicanum* (Caley, i. 563) says that he found the monastery "*spoliatum et ruinosum*," and therefore rebuilt it. He also changed its constitution, by introducing secular priests, of whom many were married to lawful wives, and who were very little different in their way of living to other secular Christians. This state of things went on till 1022, when Cnut, as Leland says, "for ill lyvynge expellyd secular clerks, and by the counsell of Wolstane (Wulfstan), Bysshope of Wurcestar, bringethe in monkes." The monks introduced by Cnut were of the Benedictine rule, or Black monks, as Parker calls them in his "Rhythmical History of the Abbey."

This change was effected about the same time in many other places in England, but was not generally popular, and certainly was not so in Gloucester. Abbot Parker, in his rhyming account of the founding of the abbey, says that in 1030

> " A lord of great puissance, named Ulfine Le Rewe,
> Was enjoyned by (the Pope) for ever to finde
> Satisfying for the seaven priests that he slew,
> 7 monkes for them to pray world without minde."

Mr Hope, in his "Notes on the Benedictine Abbey of St. Peter at Gloucester," 1897, p. 2, says: "The Benedictines thus introduced by Cnut do not seem to have been a success, and after an existence of thirty-seven years under a weak Abbot, whose long rule was marked by great decay of discipline, the '*Memoriale*' (Dugdale, i. 564) says: 'God permitted them to be extirpated, and the monastery in which they were established to be devoured by the fiercest flames, and the very foundations and buildings to be rent asunder, razed to the ground, and utterly destroyed.'"

"The monastery was next taken in hand by Aldred, Bishop of Worcester, who in 1058 re-established the monks. He also began to build a new church from the foundations, and dedicated it in honour of St. Peter."*

* So says the MS. Lives of the Abbots in the Library of Queen's College, Oxford.

"Until now the monastery seems to have occupied the same site throughout its chequered history; but the '*Memoriale*' states that Aldred began the new church 'a little further from the place where it had first stood, and nearer to the side of the city.'"

The language of these authorities is quite plain, but the interpretation thereof is not so evident. As Professor Freeman said: "By the time when the oldest church, of which we have any part remaining, came into being, the Roman Wall, or at least this corner of it, must have pretty well passed away." It seems clear that the "*side of the city*" cannot refer to the Roman Wall. To quote Professor Freeman again: "The existing church is something more than near to the Roman Wall. It actually stands over its north-west corner."

"Even under Aldred's auspices the monastery did not altogether flourish. But this time it was through the fault of Aldred himself, for, on his translation to York in 1060, he retained very many of the possessions of the abbey that had been pledged to him on account of his expenses in repairing and re-edifying the church."

In 1072, Wilstan (Wulstan), the Abbot consecrated by Aldred in 1058, died, and was succeeded by Serlo, who found the convent reduced to two monks and eight novices. Through his energy the monastery increased to such an extent that in about fifteen years' time it became necessary to rebuild the monastery.

This rebuilding was begun exactly thirty-one years after Aldred had built his church, *de novo* and *a fundamentis*. Why was this necessary? Professor Freeman says: "The reason is not very far to seek for any one who has really mastered the history of architecture during the eleventh century. . . . The simple fact is that the Norman prelates pulled down and rebuilt the English churches, mainly because they thought them too small." Further on he says: "This proves that, of the two types of church which were in use side by side in the days of the Confessor, Aldred had followed the older type. He had not conformed to the new Norman fashions, vast size among them, which were coming in after the example of the king's own church at Westminster. . . . His church was built in the Primitive Romanesque style, the style common to England, with Germany, Italy, and Burgundy, not in the newly-developed style of Northern Gaul. Therefore, neither its scale nor its style suited the ideas of Abbot Serlo.* It was condemned, and the minster that now stands was begun."

In the MS. Lives of the Abbots in Queen's College Library, Oxford, it is stated that "in A.D. 1089, on the day of the festival of the Apostles Peter and Paul, in this year were laid the foundations of the church (ecclesia) of Gloucester, the venerable man Robert, Bishop of Hereford, laying the first stone, Serlo the Abbot being in charge of the work." (So, too, Hart, i. 11.)

In August 1089 there was an earthquake, which did serious damage to the then existing building. Eleven years after this (1100), in the last year of the reign of William Rufus, "the church," as Florence of Worcester wrote, "which Abbot Serlo, of revered memory, had built from the foundations at Gloucester, was dedicated (on Sunday, July 15th) with great pomp by Samson, Bishop of Worcester; Gundulf, Bishop of Rochester; Gerard, Bishop of Hereford; and Herveas, Bishop of Bangor." This dedication under Serlo's *régime* is the last authentic record for some years.

Nothing is known exactly as to how much of the building was completed by 1100. Professor Freeman points out that eleven years was quite long enough for its building, and that there is no hint in the local chronicle of any additions being made to the building dedicated in 1100. Probably part of the church was finished for the dedication, such as the presbytery, choir, the transepts, the Abbot's cloister, the chapter-house, and the greater part, at any rate, of the nave.

The nave, though so different in scale as compared with the original choir, must have been built very early in the twelfth century, and, like the rest of the building, originally had a wooden roof.

In 1101 or 1102 damage was done to the building by fire, notably the chapter-house, and again in 1122. Possibly in this latter fire the nave roof was destroyed, and of this fire the piers in the nave show traces. Of the same date must be much of the strengthening masonry in the crypt, the Prior's lodging, the chapel, and the slype beneath it.

The whole of the Abbey buildings were surrounded by Abbot Peter with a stone wall, and the necessary gates—viz.

* Formerly a canon of the Church of Avranches, and afterwards a monk in the Church of Mont St. Michel.

HISTORY OF THE BUILDING

the great gatehouse on the west, another on the south, and a third more to the east. All these can be identified from the small plan of the monastic buildings, reproduced (p. 103), by permission of Mr F. S. Waller. The Saxon Chronicle tells us that in 1122, while the monks were singing mass, fire burst out from the upper part of the steeple, and burnt the whole monastery. Some time between 1164 and 1179 one of the western towers, probably the south-west tower, fell down. Fire in 1190 is said to have destroyed the greater part of the city, as well as almost all the buildings in the outer court. Helias, the sacrist, also made new stalls for the monks in the choir. Of these Early English stalls, a fragment has been thoughtfully and carefully preserved behind the seat of the Canon in residence.

In 1222 we learn from Hart, i. 25, that the great eastern tower was built under the direction of Helias of Hereford, the sacrist. Of this tower no traces now remain. Helias built his superstructure on the Norman work that we see in the nave.

The Early English Lady Chapel was said to have been built between the years 1224-1227 by Ralph of Wylington, and Olympias his wife, and endowed with lands.

The church was dedicated again in 1239, in Abbot Foliot's time, by Walter of Cantelupe, "the patriot prelate who, six-and-twenty years later, stood by Earl Simon on the day of martyrdom at Evesham."

Three years after the dedication in 1242 alterations in the triforium of the nave were made, and the stone vaulting was done by the monks themselves. It was a very laudable object, but they effectually spoiled the nave. The same year saw the beginning of the rebuilding of the south-west tower, and it was finished before 1246. If this was the tower that collapsed in 1170, the monks would seem to have somewhat neglected their duty to the fabric. The Norman refectory or "frater" was demolished in 1246, and the new one begun. This building stood to the north of the cloisters, and was pulled down at the Dissolution. Of the Early English infirmary or "farmery" traces remain near the Bishop's Palace.

In this place we may refer incidently to Gloucester Hall, Oxford, which college was founded in 1283 as a residence for thirteen monks, to be chosen out of the brotherhood at Gloucester, and sent to study at Oxford. The hall was empowered later on to receive students from other Benedictine foundations, and the buildings were enlarged for this purpose in 1298.

Fire again ravaged the Abbey and its precincts in 1300, on the feast of the Epiphany. "It began in a timbered house in the great court, from which it spread to the small bell-tower, the great camera, and the cloister" (Hope, 36). Mr Hope thinks this bell-tower was either a single western tower, as formerly there was at Hereford, or else a Norman north-west tower, and that the great camera was part of the Abbot's house, now the Deanery. Professor Freeman thinks that the small bell-tower or *parvum campanile* was so called as being less in height than the south-west tower rebuilt in 1245-6.

In this same fire the Norman dorter or dormitory suffered considerable damage. It was pulled down three years later, and a new one, which took ten years to build, was opened for use in 1313, after being blessed and sprinkled with holy water by the Bishop of St. David's. 1318 is a date of importance in the history of the Abbey. John Thokey, Abbot from 1307-1329, made many changes. He reconstructed the south aisle of the nave to save the south side from collapse. The windows on the outside have been restored, but the buttresses have been very little touched. Most of the tracery in the windows of the aisles and chapels of the choir, and the triforium of the choir, date back to his time.

Thokey, between 1316-1329 built the new camera of the Abbot, beside the infirmary garden (Hart, i. 55).

Thokey's successor, Wygmore, carried out the works planned previously, and in 1331-1337 the south transept was recased, and vaulted practically as we see it to-day, in the style now known as Perpendicular. Part of the front of the Deanery is presumably of the same date, though many later alterations have been made in it. Wygmore also built the double screen (*vide* p. 44) which separated the nave from the choir. "Parts of it," says Mr Hope, "are worked up in the present screen," and he quotes Hart, i. 47, to show that Wygmore was buried in 1337, "before the Salutation of the Blessed Mary in the entry of the quire on the south side, which he himself constructed with the pulpitum (or loft) in the same place."

The transformation of the Norman minster had thus begun. In the days of Adam de Staunton (1337-1357) the great vault of the choir was made at a great expense, together with the stalls on the Priors' side—*i.e.* the north side.

The oblations at the tomb of Edward II. rendered much of his extensive work practicable, as the funds of the Abbey were becoming exhausted.

Thomas Horton (1351-1377) finished the work, comprising the high altar, with the presbytery, the stalls on the Abbot's side, or south side of the choir. (Hart, i. 49.)

He also caused to be made the images and tabernacle work at the entrance of the choir on the north side, and in the six years, ending with 1374, he completed the casing of the north transept, defraying the greater part of the cost himself (£444, 0s. 2d. out of a total sum of £781, 0s. 2d.).

Horton also built "the Abbot's chapel near the garden of the infirmary, the covered camera of the monks' hostelry, and the great hall in the court, where the king afterwards held his Parliament in 1378." (Hart, i. 48, 50.)

The present cloister, as far as the door of the chapter-house, is also his work.

This important work was for many years unfinished, but was completed by Froucester in the years 1381-1407. As Leland says, "he made the cloyster a right goodly and sumptuous piece of worke."

In the one hundred and thirty years that elapsed between the finishing of the cloisters and the Dissolution many further important changes took place, both in the interior and in the exterior of the fabric.

John Morwent (1421-1437), utterly destroyed the west front, with its two towers, which, in the opinion of many, may have been those counterparts at Tewkesbury. To him also is credited, mainly on Leland's authority, the insertion of the south porch.

Abbot Seabroke (1450-1457) took down the tower as far as the Norman piers, and built the present beautiful structure. He died before it was finished, and Robert Tully, one of the monks of the monastery, carried out the work, as the inscription on the wall in the interior (*vide* p. 63) testifies.

Before the tower was complete, the present Lady Chapel

(which was finished before 1500) was begun by Abbot Hanley, and finished by Abbot Farley.

John the Baptist's Chapel is usually ascribed to Abbot John Browne (or Newton), from the similarity of his initials to those of the saint.

The eastern bay of the chapter-house dates back to Abbot Hanley's time—*i.e.* between 1457-1472.

In 1540 Henry VIII. sent his commissioners, and they demanded the surrender of the Abbey to the king. This cannot have been a surprise to any of the monks who were in the Abbey at the time. As far back as 1534 they had all been compelled to take the oath by which they acknowledged the king as supreme head of the Church of England, and denied that any foreign bishop had any authority in these realms.

The monks, too, had seen the smaller monasteries in Gloucester dissolved two years before, and the more thoughtful of them must have foreseen that it was a mere question of time for the greedy king to absorb the larger monasteries as well.

Abbot Parker's tomb, and also that of King Osric, practically date themselves, and of the same period are presumably the gateway into Palace Yard, and part of the Abbot's lodging on the site of the present Bishop's Palace. From Leland we learn that the south gate—*i.e.* King Edward's gate—is of the same date, having been rebuilt by Osborne the cellarer.

The library, and the set of rooms beneath it, now used as vestry and practice-room for the choir, are perhaps the latest additions to the buildings.

At the Dissolution the Abbey which had "existed for more than eight centuries under different forms, in poverty and in wealth, in meanness and in magnificence, in misfortune and success, finally succumbed to the royal will. The day came, and that a drear winter day, when its last mass was sung, its last censer waved, its last congregation bent in rapt and lowly adoration before the altar there; and, doubtless, as the last tones of that day's evensong died away in the vaulted roof, there were not wanting those who lingered in the solemn stillness of the old massive pile, and who, as the lights disappeared one by one, felt that there was a void which could never be filled, because their old abbey, with its beautiful services, its frequent means of grace, its hospitality to strangers, and its loving care for God's poor, had passed away like a morning dream, and was gone for ever." (Hart, iii. 49.)

The charter of Henry VIII. founding the see is too long to quote *in extenso*, but it stated that "Whereas the great convent or monastery, which, whilst still in being, was called the monastery of St. Peter of Gloucester, ... and all and singular its manors, ... and possessions, for certain special and urgent causes were, by Gabriel Moreton, Prior of the said abbey or monastery and the convent thereof, lately given and granted to us and our heirs for ever. ... We, being influenced by divine goodness, and desiring above all things, that true religion, and the true worship of God may not only not be abolished, but entirely restored to the primitive and genuine rule of simplicity; and that all those enormities may be corrected into which the lives and profession of the monks for a long time had deplorably lapsed, have, as far as human frailty will permit, endeavoured to the utmost that for the future the pure word of God may be taught in that place, good discipline preserved. ..."

The charter goes on to say that, "considering the site of the said late monastery in which many famous monuments of our renowned ancestors, Kings of England, are erected is a very fit and proper place ... we have decreed that the site of the said monastery be an episcopal see. ... We also will and ordain that the said Dean and Prebendaries, and their successors, shall for ever hereafter be called the Dean and Chapter of the Holy and Individed Trinity of Gloucester." Henry also assigned to the Bishop all the premises formerly occupied by the Abbot.

In 1576 the fabric seems to have been in want of considerable repair, and in 1616, when Dr Laud was Dean, it was said of it that "there was scarcely a church in England so much in decay." The Dean procured an Act of the Chapter, by which the sum of £60 per annum was to be allowed for repairs.

In the time of the civil war it suffered less than might have been expected. It was subsequently in danger of total destruction from the machinations of some persons, who are said "to have agreed amongst themselves for their several proportions of the plunder expected out of it." The little cloisters and the Lady Chapel were begun to be pulled down, and "instruments and tackle provided for to take down the tower," but in 1657 the church was made over by grant to the mayor and burgesses at their request, and from this it is to be assumed that they wished to prevent it from possible ruin. Mr Dorney, speaking in 1653, recommends to the officers of the city then elected, "that they would, together with others, join their shoulders to hold up the stately fabric of the College Church, the great ornament of this city, which some do say is now in danger of falling."

In 1679 we find an insensate prebendary securing an order from the Chapter for destroying some of the old glass in the west window of the choir. Bishop Benson (1734-1752) spent vast sums of money on the building, and to him are due the paving of the nave, and pinnacles to the Lady Chapel, which were removed at a recent restoration. A stone screen (removed in 1820) was erected at the entrance to the choir by this energetic Bishop, and his architect, Kent, in whose hands he was, suggested the fluting of the pillars of the nave.

Fifty years ago, in 1847, under the energetic administration of Dr Jeune, the Treasurer, extensive repairs and improvements were begun by Mr F. S. Waller. The crypt was drained, concreted, and later on glazed. The grounds round the cathedral have been lowered, enlarged, and laid out, and the drainage has been properly done. Of the restorations during the last fifty years mention has been made in detail in the description of the various parts of the building that have been restored, and there is no need to repeat.

Restoration is a cause of much strife, and in the hands of many architects it means destruction of the original features of the building. Gloucester has suffered somewhat at the hands of Sir Gilbert Scott, but probably not a tithe of what would have been inflicted upon it had Wyatt been turned loose with an absolutely free hand. Mr Waller, writing in 1890, said: "Forty years ago everything not 'Gothic' (the fashion of the day) was destroyed; but were it possible now to reinstate the Chapter-House book-cases, the Renaissance Reredos of the Choir, Wygmore's pulpit, the aisle screens, the remains of the Rood Loft, and the Choir fittings, and to put them all back—odd mixture as they would be—to the positions they occupied in 1727, few would be found to object, even though the replacement of the monuments on the columns of the nave became one of the conditions."—Truly "*Tempora mutantur,*" and fortunately *nos et mutamur in illis.*

Dedication.—The building of Osric was dedicated to St. Peter by Theodore, Archbishop of Canterbury, and Bosel, Bishop of Worcester. When Bishop Wulfstan ejected the secular canons, and brought in his Benedictine monks, he reconsecrated it to St. Peter and St. Paul.

Bishop Aldred after building *de novo* re-dedicated the church to St. Peter, as the chief of the apostles. Abbot Serlo seems to have remembered the earlier dedication to St. Peter and St. Paul, for he caused the foundation-stone to be laid in 1089 on the festival of those two apostles in June, but his dedication in 1100 was to St. Peter. Both St. Peter and St. Paul are now represented among the statues on the front of the south porch. After the dissolution of the monastery Henry VIII. ascribed the Cathedral Church to the Holy and Individed Trinity.

The Cathedral is traditionally by many called "St. Peter's," and by some "The Abbey Church," but this, of course, is quite inaccurate.

Apropos of the question of the dedication, the arms of the see may be briefly considered.

The original arms were Azure, two keys in saltire, or.

By the fifteenth century the sword for St. Paul had become incorporated with the crossed keys, and it is found upon the bells and also on the east side of the organ case. At the Dissolution the arms were Gules, two keys in saltire surmounted by a sword in pale, argent. Brown Willis, in 1727, wrote that "the old arms of this see as used 100 years ago, were three chevronels, the middle one charged with a mitre, but the bishops now give *Azure, two keys in saltire, or.*"

CHAPTER II

THE EXTERIOR

OF the building as originally constructed, practically the whole, as far as the outline is concerned, may be said to remain as it was at the beginning of the twelfth century. The massive Norman nave, the slype or covered passage that is between the Deanery and the north-west wall of the cathedral, the two transepts with their turrets, the choir with its various chapels and aisles, the chapter-house, and the Abbot's cloister, are all parts of the original building, although later additions have partly concealed them.

In Mr Waller's "Notes and Sketches of Gloucester Cathedral"* a very interesting view is given of the cathedral stripped of every addition of a later date than the original structure, and by his permission it is here reproduced.

With reference to this sketch Mr Waller says :

"This sketch is given to shew what is left of the old Abbey Church of the twelfth century, and looking to the fact that it was not too reliable a structure to begin with, as regards foundation and settlements (not forgetting the "earthquake"), it certainly is wonderful what extraordinary liberties have been taken with the old fabric, and what really great risks have been incurred. Look at and consider this sketch with reference to the building as it now stands, and excepting in the aisles of the Choir, the north aisle of the Nave, and part of the Chapter-Room, where the original vaulting remains, it will be seen that it is a *mere shell*, the walls have been pulled about in the most reckless manner, and in all directions, and in the Choir they have actually been pared down and an outer casing has been entirely removed—large pieces have been cut out of the piers for the introduction of monuments (mediæval, not modern!), window heads have been removed to make way for the more recent works, and nearly the whole of the Cathedral has been covered with a sort of appliqué work of mullions and tracery, erected chiefly in the fourteenth century (see sketch on plate 4). The large central Tower (forty feet square on the leads) has been built on the old Norman walls ; new walls, new vaulting, and new roofs have been erected on old foundations ; and, strange to say, scarcely a settlement of any kind can be seen in any of the building operations which have been

* This is now out of print.

undertaken since 1200! It is not too much to say that a man of the present day who would even suggest such works as have been here successfully accomplished, would be most severely condemned; but in those days the Abbots had only themselves to please, there were no well-educated reporters and writers to discuss their doings in morning papers: they felt, therefore, quite at their ease, hoping for the best, and in this instance

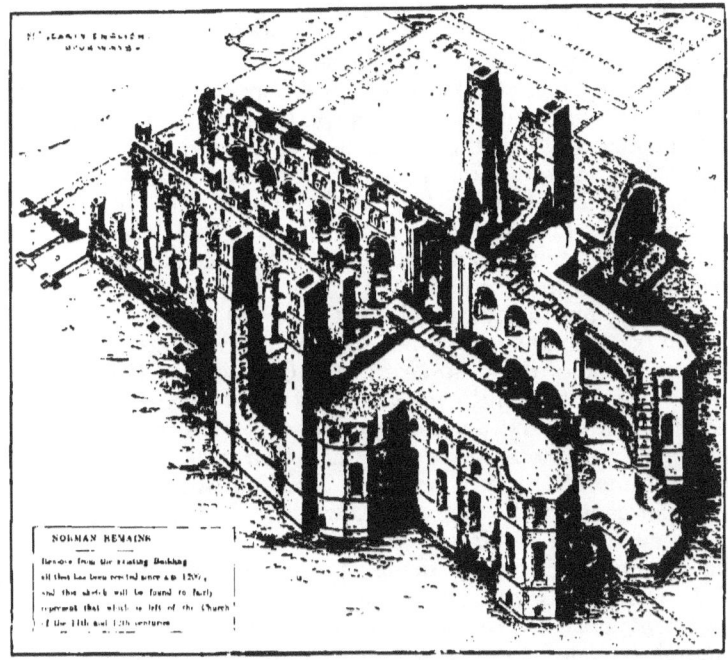

[From a Drawing by F. S. Waller, F.R.I.B.A.

succeeding admirably, not only as regards their own wishes and intentions, but in leaving for posterity a splendid architectural history in stone."

"The plan of the building is cruciform, and consists of a Nave and Choir, with Aisles on the north and south sides of each; North and South Transepts, at the intersection of which with the Choir rises the Tower; and at intervals round the Choir Aisles are four small apsidal Chapels. At the east end is the Lady-Chapel, prior to the erection of which, a fifth Chapel, similar in form and dimensions to the other four, existed at the east end; as may be seen in the plan of the Crypt."

The whole building, according to Professor Willis, is full of peculiar fancies, which all appear to be characteristic of a school of masons who were extremely skilful, and glad of an opportunity of showing their skill. The mediæval masons, he thinks, were "perfectly practical and most ingenious men; they worked experimentally: if their buildings were strong enough, there they stood; if they were too strong, they also stood; but if they were too weak they gave way, and they put props and built the next stronger." That was their science—and very good practical science it was—but in many cases they imperilled their work, and gave trouble to future restorers.

The arrangement of the buildings differs in one very essential point from almost every other in the kingdom. The cloisters and the claustral buildings were, as a rule, on the south side of the church, for the sake of shelter, and also of sunshine. At Gloucester they are on the north side of the church, the reason being (according to Mr Fosbroke) that when Aldred laid the new foundations farther south, the cloisters found themselves on the north side.

Dallaway has said very truly that "Few churches in England exhibit so complete a school of Gothic in all its gradations from the time of the Conquest as the Cathedral of Gloucester." This is true with the exception that of "Decorated" architecture there are but few examples, and it is probable that very little new work was done in connection with this cathedral until the monastery became vastly enriched by Abbot Thokey's policy in causing the body of Edward II. to be brought from Berkeley Castle for interment in his abbey. It is said that the amount of offerings made at the tomb during the reign of Edward III. was enough to have entirely rebuilt the abbey. In consequence of this the Cathedral is full of some of the finest examples of the styles known as "Transition from Decorated to Perpendicular" (anticipative Perpendicular) and pure "Perpendicular"—a style which, in Professor Willis's opinion, originated at Gloucester. From every side there is something to interest the careful observer.

As a rule, visitors see it first from the south side, and the south-west general view is one of the best, equalled, but not surpassed, by that from the north-west. The north view from the Great Western Railway, with the school playing-fields in the foreground, makes a striking picture, but it is more sombre than the picture formed by the south front. Viewed from the north-west corner of the cloister-garth, the pile is seen perhaps at its best. From this point it is

[*Photochrom Co. Ltd., Photo.*]

THE CATHEDRAL FROM THE SOUTH-WEST.

easy to study so much of the varied architecture of the whole, and with little effort to transport the mind back for a space of four hundred years. The eye first rests upon the turf of the garth, now tastefully laid out after many years of

Photochrom Co. Ltd., Photo.]
THE CATHEDRAL, FROM THE NORTH-WEST
CORNER OF THE CLOISTERS.

comparative neglect. Flanking the garth on every side are the exquisite windows of the Cloister—a cloister which no other can surpass. Above the Cloister will be seen on the eastern side the sober, impressive Norman work of the Chapter-House in which so much of our English history has been made. To the south of this is the Library, built close against the walls of the north transept, which tower above, and lead the eye upward to the great tower which, "in the middest of the church," crowns the whole.

Looking for a moment at the Norman windows in the north aisle, one sees how they have been altered in their details since they were built, though their bold outline remains the same. The windows in the clerestory tell the tale of a later time, probably that of Abbot Morwent.

The **West Front**.—Compared with many others of our cathedral fronts, this front may seem to be of less interest, but it has the great beauty of simplicity, which prevents it, when viewed in the foreground, from killing the rest of the picture. The buttresses of the great window are ingeniously pierced, so as not to cut off the light; and the parapets, also of pierced or open work, should be carefully noted.

Plain transoms cross the lights, whereas in the inside the tracery and cusping is elaborate. This will be noted also in the east window of the choir and elsewhere.

Of the western towers which formerly existed no traces now remain. The north-west tower, owing to badly-made foundations, collapsed in the latter half of the twelfth century between 1163-1179.

A south-west tower was begun in 1242 by Walter de St. John, Prior at the time, and subsequently Abbot for a few weeks, and it was finished by his successor, John de la Feld.

When Abbot Morwent altered the west end and front, the western towers disappeared altogether. This front was restored carefully, where necessary, in 1874.

The **South Porch**.—This portion of the building is the work of Morwent, who was Abbot from 1421-1437. The rich front of what Bonner called "Saracenic work," was formerly disfigured by an uninteresting dial with the motto *Pereunt et imputantur*. This was removed at the Restoration, when the canopies were restored, and niches filled with statues by Redfern. Over the doorway in the centre, stand St. Peter and St. Paul, and the four Evangelists. Below are King Osric and Abbot Serlo, the two founders of the Abbey Church. The four figures in the niches of the buttresses represent St. Jerome, St. Ambrose, St. Augustine, and St. Gregory. The windows of the porch have been formed by piercing the internal tracery. This has a very curious effect when viewed

THE EXTERIOR

from the inside. From the outside the windows do not seem unusual.

The Porch was in such a very ruinous state, that it was

The Tower from the Palace-yard

(Drawn by E. J. Burrow.

scarcely possible to use any of the old stone on the outside. Within, the old work can be seen, and the bosses are worthy of attention. Over the porch is an unfinished parvise. The doors are very good specimens of fifteenth-century work.

The **South Transept** (or St. Andrew's Aisle), as far as the walls are concerned, is thought by some to have been built by

Serlo, but there have been so many alterations in the exterior that it is difficult to say anything with certainty. Fosbroke, writing at the end of last century, noted that there was an inscription on the outside wall making mention of one William Pipard, who was sheriff of the county about sixty years after Serlo's time. The windows have been enlarged and much altered, and later tracery has been inserted.

In spite of the many alterations and some restoration, the south front of this transept contains much interesting Norman work, which has been re-used in a very clever way. The square flanking towers, with their later spires, the arcading over the head of the window, and the graceful curve in the battlement are all worthy of attention, and will serve to confuse visitors before they realise that the Norman architecture is concealed under a later casing, and that there is a great deal of old work re-used in the new.

There is a curious buttress, too, which goes across the west window of this transept to strengthen the south-west corner of the great tower. In fact, the south side of the church is the only side that, as builders say, has "settled" at all.

In 1867 a Roman tesselated pavement was discovered near the south front of this transept.

The **Tower**.—Of all the exterior beauties, the most striking is the beautiful and graceful tower. Placed where it is, almost in the centre of the long line of the nave, continued in the choir and Lady Chapel, at the point where the transept line intersects it, it is the chief feature of the massive pile. All else seems to be grouped with a view to the enhancing of the effect of the central position of the tower. The other members of the building seem merely to be steps, by means of which approach can be made to it. It is the grandest and most impressive feature of the outside. No matter from whence one looks at it, the charm is there. Seen from the gardens in the side streets close by when the pear-trees are in bloom, or in the full blaze of a hot summer day, or again later in the autumn when the leaves are beginning to turn, or, better still, in snow time, it is always full of beauty. On a bright hot day the pinnacles seem so far off in the haze as to suggest a dream of fairyland. On a wet day, after a shower, the tower has the appearance of being so close at hand that it almost seems to speak. Viewed by moonlight, the tower has an unearthly look,

THE CATHEDRAL IN 1727.   [From an old Print.

which cannot well be described. The tower is 225 feet high to the top of the pinnacles, and the effect of it is extremely fine. From the main cornice upwards, the whole of the stonework is open, and composed of what at a distance appears to be delicate tracery, and mullions, and crocketed pinnacles.

It is, in all probability, the third tower that has been built since Aldred's time. There are piers still remaining of the Norman tower erected by Serlo in the years that elapsed between 1089 and 1100; and, as we are told in the "Saxon Chronicle," that in 1122 a fire which originated in the upper part of the steeple burnt the whole monastery, it must be inferred that the superstructure was of wood. A hundred years later it is known that the great eastern tower was built with the help of Helias of Hereford. This tower was in great part taken down by the monk Tully, and rebuilt in the Perpendicular style in the time of Abbot Seabroke (1450-1457).

The **Bells** at Gloucester are peculiarly interesting from the fact of their age, and from the fact that they escaped the clutches of the despoilers at the time of the Dissolution. The truth of the matter seems to be that all the "Churche goods, money, juells, plate, vestments, ornaments, and bells" had been inventoried and handed over to the king's commissioners in Bishop Hooper's time. The commissioners returned to the Dean and Chapter "to and for the use and behouf of the seid Churche, one chalys being silver and whole gilte without a paten waying xi oz. and also one grete bell whereuppon the cloke strykithe, and eight other grete bells whereupon the chyme goethe hangynge in the towre there within the seid church save and surely to be kept untill the King's Majesty's pleasure shall be therein further knowen." This was dated May 27th, 1553, and as the king died within three months his pleasure in the matter was never "further knowen," and Gloucester rejoices still in its bells.

The chimes * play four tunes, which are changed every other day. The first tune was composed by Dr Jefferies in 1791; the second by Dr Hayes, who died 1777; the third by Dr Malchair, 1760-1770; and the fourth by Dr Stevens. The composers of the second and fourth tunes were both natives of Gloucester, and at one time choristers in the cathedral.

* They have lately been undergoing repair, and will soon be in working order again.

THE EXTERIOR

"The shape of the east end of the old Church, as will be seen by a reference to the ground plan and plan of the Crypt, is partly round and partly polygonal; round as regards the outer wall of the main building and the inside and outside

[Photochrom Co. Ltd., Photo.]
THE SOUTH PORCH (SINCE THE RESTORATION).

of the small Chapels in the Crypt, but polygonal in the interior walls of the main building in the Crypt; whereas on the ground-floor the main building and the Chapels are all polygonal.* An examination of the remains of the Eastern Arches, as seen above the last Norman piers eastward of the Choir, shows the direction of the lines distinctly, following as they do the lines of the Crypt below, but with less heavy construction. The whole of the edifice, with the exception of the Lady Chapel and the Cloisters, remains, as regards general outline, as it stood in the early part of the twelfth century. (See illustration, p. 15.) The Nave with its large circular columns, the slype adjoining the Deanery (probably indicating the extent westwards of the Norman Towers prior to the erection of the present west end), the North and South Transepts, with their Turrets at the west and east angles, the Choir and its Aisles and Chapels, the Chapter-House and Abbot's Cloister, although more or less masked by later additions, are all parts of the original building."

The method of joining the Lady Chapel to the choir is best noticed from the outside. It is a piece of exceedingly clever and graceful construction, and there is the minimum of obstruction to the light passing through to the east window, and the maximum of support to the elliptical east window.

Another interesting feature in this part of the exterior is the construction of the two passages—chiefly of re-used Norman work—which make up the greater part of the so-called Whispering Gallery—*i.e.* the passage connecting the north and the south triforium of the choir.

One of the distinguishing features of the exterior of the building is the variety and arrangement of the battlements and pinnacles. Bishop Benson did his best to spoil the effect of those on the Lady Chapel by removing the upper part of the parapet and by substituting other pinnacles. These have been restored, but the east-end pinnacles do not seem quite in keeping with Gloucester. Viewing the Lady Chapel from the north side, the play of light through the windows on the south side has a very grand effect. Under the east end of the Lady Chapel is a passage which has given rise to much speculation in bygone times.

The **Lady Chapel** at the time of its erection was carried

* James Fergusson, writing to Mr Waller on the above subject, says: "It is curious that polygonal forms should be used in this country in the eleventh century, whilst at Caen and on the Continent generally circular forms prevailed well into the twelfth century."

THE EXTERIOR

out to the farthest limit of the land possessed by the Abbey, shown on the plan at F.F. As the east wall of the chapel was actually on the western boundary wall the passage was made to give access from the north to the south of the grounds, without the need of going right round the precincts by the west front.

Modern improvements have increased the facilities for studying and admiring the building. In 1847-8 the garden was laid out, and from it the outside can easily be carefully examined.

S. B. Bolas & Co., Photo.]
PISCINA IN THE TRIFORIUM.

CHAPTER III

THE INTERIOR

"THE most detailed description of architectural works must fail to convey to the mind so clear and correct an impression, as the graphic representation of the objects themselves does to the eye; and the more laboured the attempt to describe in words the position, the arrangement, the form and magnitude of the several parts, the more the picture becomes confused, and the less likely to answer the purpose" (*Quart. Rev.*, No. 37, 179).

How far the above statement is of universal application is not a matter to be here discussed, but it will be appreciated to the full by anyone who attempts to describe, within definite and narrow limits, the many beauties of one of our finest cathedrals, such as Gloucester undoubtedly is.

To fully appreciate the beauty of the cathedral, it must be studied under different aspects and at different times. Much will depend upon the mood of the visitor, much, too, upon the time of day. The Lady Chapel at 7 A.M. is quite a different thing from the Lady Chapel at 10.30 or 12 noon, though always beautiful. The same holds good with the choir and the nave. A slanting light through the south clerestory playing fitfully upon the lace-work of the north side of the choir, or the sturdy pillars of the ever-impressive nave, gives a charm that cannot be described.

How grand a sight, too, it is when the nave is almost in darkness—save for eight or ten small jets of light overhead—to see the choir lighted up, with the organ standing out in strong relief against the blaze of light below and behind it, and now and then a gleam of light showing through as the door under the screen is opened.

Then, again, note and study the marvellous effects of sound in the building. Listen, if possible, from the Lady Chapel, to an anthem by some old composer; listen to Bach's G minor

Photochrom Co. Ltd., Photo.]
THE NAVE, LOOKING EAST.

fugue from the triforium of the choir, and hear the echoes rolling from pier to pier; listen to the Hallelujah Chorus sung on some great festival service in the nave, or some simple well-known hymn sung by close upon 3000 people, and the listener will have some idea of the effect that mere sound, taken as such, can produce.

The sound of Stainer's Gregorian *Miserere*, sung entirely unaccompanied, as heard from the great west door, is grand in the extreme. It needs but little imagination to take oneself back, say, four hundred years, and picture the monks singing the very same Psalm.

The tiles in an ancient building are always of interest, and Gloucester contains many that are worth inspection. There are some in the choir and its chapels, and there are some in the Lady Chapel; others may be found near Raikes' monument, exposed to view in the south aisle. There are also some in the south-east chapel of the triforium of the choir. The chapter-house tiles are modern (Minton), but were made after the tiles that were in existence there.

The nave was originally tiled, and specimens have been found when excavations have been made. In the days that are to come, possibly, the Georgian flooring may be taken up, and the tiles now hidden from view will be revealed in places where they have not been broken up, where graves have been dug in the nave and aisles.

Perhaps the weakest point in the cathedral is the modern glass. There is much that shows careful work and thought, but there has been no systematic controlling spirit at work to suggest, to guide, or to check. The chief blots, too, are the so-called memorial windows, and the reason is not hard to find. It is well put by Mr Ruskin, who, in his "Seven Lamps of Architecture," says: "The peculiar manner of selfish and impious ostentation, provoked by the glassmakers for a stimulus to trade, of putting up painted windows to be records of private affection, instead of universal religion, is one of the worst, because most plausible and proud, hypocrisies of our day."

Just imagine the difference in the south aisle, for instance, if there had been a scheme carefully planned beforehand for the windows, instead of the threefold, but haphazard, process of a window offered, a window accepted, a window put up, and no questions asked as to designer or artist. Imagine what the effect might, or would, have been, had the windows, as a set, been designed by Burne-Jones and executed by William Morris, or by other competent artists. Now, unfortunately, these two great artists are dead, and Gloucester has not a single specimen of their work.

The **Nave** as it is (174 feet by $34\frac{1}{4}$ feet long, 67 feet 7 inches high) is quite unique, and differs considerably from other Norman naves, such as are to be found in the cathedrals at Ely, Norwich, or Peterborough, and in the neighbouring abbey churches at Tewkesbury, and Great Malvern.

The unique features here are the great height of the massive circular columns, fourteen in number, and the consequently dwarfed triforium or gallery running over the main arches. There are traces to be seen of the original Norman clerestory under the Perpendicular windows, and, judging from this, the height of the clerestory, as originally constructed, must have been but little less than that of the piers in the nave.

This Norman clerestory was altered at the same time that the roof of the nave was vaulted—viz. in 1242, in the time of Henry Foliot. This work was done by the monks themselves, who thought, as Professor Willis suggests, that they could do it better than common workmen. Their work is made of a light and porous kind of stone, treated with plaster on the under-side, and it was rendered necessary by the previous roof, which was of wood, having been destroyed by fire in 1190. Of this fire the piers certainly show the traces to this day, all having become reddened and slightly calcined. To make the new clerestory the whole of the original Norman work over the arcade of the triforium was removed, with the exception of the jambs of the side-lights (which extended beyond the arches of the triforium) and the wall between them.

Mr Gambier Parry has also truly said that this work "was not an artistic success. They cut and maimed the features of the fine old Norman clerestory, and placed their thin weak work too low, destroying all the original grandeur of effect. . . . Here in this first pointed vaulting was a grievous and irreparable injury, destroying all sense of proportion throughout the building."

The vaulting shafts and the abaci are of Purbeck marble, and the capitals are of stone, as are also the corbels, bases,

S. B. Bolas & Co., Photo.]
THE NAVE AND NORTH AISLE.

mouldings, and bosses. All the stonework was formerly painted. Mr Waller, who carried out the repairs to the nave, had excellent opportunities of seeing what was left of the painting underneath the many coats of whitewash; he wrote in 1856: "The painting may be thus generally described. The hollow of the abacus of the capitals was red, the lower member of the same green; the whole of the bell red, the leaves alternately green and yellow, with the stalks, running down, of the same colours, into the red bell of the capital. The vertical mouldings between the marble shafts were red and blue alternately; the lower shafts green and blue, with red in the hollows, and the foliage on these also is green and yellow. Some of the horizontal mouldings are partly coloured also. The bosses in the groining are yellow and green, as in the capitals. All the colouring, which was very rich, was effected with water colours; in one instance only has any gold been discerned, and that was upon one of the bosses in the roof."

The fourteen piers are 30 feet 7 inches in height, or about twice the height of those at Norwich.*

The Norman piers have round or cushioned capitals. Their arches have zig-zag work in the outer moulding, and a double cable in the soffit. A cable moulding runs along just above the arches. The grotesque heads on the arches in the nave are said to represent the various mummeries of the Anglo-Saxon gleemen. A frieze of such may be seen at Kilpeck Church, in Herefordshire. It will be noticed how the cable moulding above the arches passes round some of the western vaulting shafts, and is cut away for those at the eastmost end of the nave.

Martin in his "Natural History of England" says: "The only blemish on the church is the enormous size of the pillars in the body of it, which are much too large in proportion to their height, and *would have been reduced to a proper size*, chiefly at the cost of the late Bishop (Benson), had it not been thought that it would have weakened them too much.

Bishop Benson's architect (Mr Kent), proposed to "flute" the columns, but, finding that the pillars consisted of a stone casing filled with rubble, he changed his plans.

* They have practically been shortened 10 inches by their plinths being concealed by the pavement put down in 1740. Their circumference is 21 feet 7 inches, and the distance from pier to pier about 12 feet 6 inches.

The **West End** of the nave, as also the corresponding portions of the two aisles, was pulled down and reconstructed by Abbot Morewent (1421-1437) in the style known as Perpendicular. It is uncertain whether Morwent's work was built on the same foundation line as the previously existing Norman work. Some have thought that he lengthened the original nave to the extent of one bay. Mr Hope considers that he curtailed it somewhat, and that the present Deanery building was similarly shortened. Anyone who will take the trouble to space out with a compass the distance between the centres of the piers in the nave on the plan will be inclined to fall in with this suggestion.

Abbot Morwent, according to Leland, intended, "if he had lived, to have made the whole body of the church of like worke." It is a matter for rejoicing that he was not spared to carry out his intentions. His work, though it has been censured, is, as Mr Waller points out, exceedingly good of its kind. Morwent may have found the west end in danger of falling, just as the towers that flanked the Norman west front had collapsed in the twelfth century.

How Morwent would have made the whole body of the church "of like worke" is another matter for speculation. Would he have kept the Norman piers in their present position, and revaulted the roof after the model of his vaulting in the second bay from the west end, or would he have diminished the number of piers so as to give a distance between them equal to the space between the west wall and the first pier he erected? It is difficult to realise how such a herculean task would have been carried out with safety to the fabric.

As to the work demolished by Morwent to make room for his own, it is only possible to hazard the conjecture that the original west front of Gloucester was something like that of the abbey at Tewkesbury, but with the additional finish of two larger western towers. As the two churches were being built almost at the same time, this conjecture seems reasonable.

The **South Aisle** of the nave was originally of Norman work, similar in style to that of the north aisle; but was remodelled and rebuilt to such an extent by Abbot Thokey, in or about the year 1318, that the piers and portions of the south wall are all that remain of the Norman work. He desired probably to preserve the Norman vaulting (similar to that yet existing in the north aisle of the nave), and as the south wall had inclined out-

S. B. Bolas & Co., Photo.]
SOUTH AISLE OF NAVE.

wards, and the whole fabric of the aisle was from this cause in danger, he erected large buttresses to prevent further settlement; but failing in this design, he was compelled to take down the Norman vaulting, and he then substituted vaulting of the same style of architecture as the buttresses he had just erected. Such great care could scarcely have been taken in those days to preserve the Norman piers only; the first object must have been to retain, for economical reasons, as much as could possibly be retained of the old aisle. It may be remarked also that the Norman piers incline in some cases as much as one foot towards the south, and the buttresses of Abbot Thokey also incline in the same direction from three to four inches in their whole height. The Abbot's buttresses, therefore, must have gone out of the perpendicular after their first erection, or else the present vaulting would show settlements, which it certainly does not.

The tracery of the windows is unusual in design, and is similar to that in a window of the chapel at Merton College, Oxford. Ball-flower mouldings adorn the aisle windows inside and out between the south door and the steps leading up to the south transept, and the same ornament is repeated in the vaulting of three of the bays and in the triforium of the choir.*

Abbot Morwent's work at the west end of this aisle is similar to that in the north aisle.

The **Monuments** in this aisle are not numerous, but are of modern historic interest. Near the west end of the nave is a statue by Silvier to Dr Jenner, who introduced the practice of vaccination. Under the west window of this aisle is an interesting wall-tablet in a canopy to John Jones, who was registrar to eight bishops of the diocese. The background is formed of files of documents, with their seals and dates exposed to view. There is taste in the colouring, and the design is effective. John Jones was M.P. for Gloucester at the exciting time of the Gunpowder Plot. He is said to have had the monument put up in his lifetime, and to have died soon after it was completed.

After passing the south door, a marble sarcophagus, with a bust upon it, will be noticed. This is to the memory of Sir G.

* Similar ornament in windows may be found at Leominster, Ledbury Church, Minsterworth, Hartbury, St. Michael's (Gloucester), and in the tower of Hereford Cathedral.

Onesiphorus Paul, Baronet, (by Sievier). His name is well-known in connection with prison reforms. Close by is a wall tablet to the widow of Sir Wm. Strachan (1770). The carving, which is very delicate and beautiful, is by Thomas Ricketts, a Gloucester sculptor of considerable skill.

There is also a monument to Rev. Thomas Stock, who, with Robert Raikes, was instrumental in opening Sunday schools.

The great West Window contains nine lights which were glazed by Wailes of Newcastle, to the memory of Dr J. H. Monk, Bishop of Gloucester from 1830 to 1856.

The **Font** is situated in the westernmost bay of the south aisle, on the site of the old Consistory Court, formerly railed off from the rest of the nave. The font being of red Aberdeen granite clashes rather with the prevailing grey stone of the building, is very heavy in appearance, and, in spite of the workmanship spent upon it, quite uninteresting. The north side contains a representation of the two prophets, Jeremiah and Ezekiel, separated by the ark; the west side has figures of St. Matthew and Daniel; the south side has figures of St. Mark and St. Luke, and the baptism of Christ in the Jordan, and the east contains the emblems of the Trinity and of baptism.

The **Windows** in this south aisle are the least interesting in the cathedral, and would seem to have been made without much consideration of the fact that they were to go where a side light would come upon them.

The five-light *west window* of the aisle is in memory of Dr Jenner and his friend Dr Baron. The subjects, appropriately enough, refer to miracles of healing, or restoring to life.

The *first south window* is to John Elliott, a solicitor, and the subjects are more or less legal. The glass is by Hardman.

The *second window* (three lights) is in memory of Miss Evans, and was put up in 1861 by Bell of Bristol. The colouring must be seen to be appreciated at its proper worth.

The *third window* is a memorial to Sir W. G. Davy, K.C.B., who died in 1856, and is buried in the cloister. The glass is by Warrington.

The *fourth window*, to the memory of Sir W. Guise, Bart., is rather kaleidoscopic in effect, owing to its being mainly an armorial window, and, secondarily, historical.

The historical portion represents the Coronation of Henry III. in Gloucester Cathedral in 1216, by Gualo (the Papal legate) and Peter de Rupibus, or des Roches, Bishop of Winchester. In the left centre light is Hubert de Burgh, Earl of Kent, and in the right is Joceline, Bishop of Bath.

The glass is by Clayton & Bell.

The *fifth window* is a memorial window to Mrs Evans. In colour it resembles the third window, and is by the same artist.

The *sixth window* is a memorial to Mrs Ellis. It is historical, but bristles with anachronisms.

The *seventh window* is a memorial (executed by Warrington) to Jeremiah Nettleton Balme.

The *eighth window* is in memory of Lieut.-Col. Sir Harry Francis Colville Darell, who died in 1853.

North Aisle.—This aisle retains its original Norman vaulting. The Norman piers, which correspond to the piers in the nave, are divided into several members, and their capitals are in some cases richly carved. In each bay the jambs and heads are of old work, filled in with Perpendicular tracing. A stone bench along the wall is also Perpendicular.

The door into the cloister at the west end of the aisle contains some very fine work. The wall is panelled on either side, and the panels are said to have formerly had paintings of the twelve apostles. The side niches and the canopy work over the door should be examined.

The door at the eastern end of the aisle by which access is gained to the cloisters and the chapter-house is also of Perpendicular work. Both of these doors have fan-vaulted recesses, like the great west door of the nave. They are so contrived that the doors may open into them and occupy the minimum of space.

Over the east door in the cloisters there were blazoned some years back the arms of the See, the Bishop, the Dean, the Canons, the Darell and Nightingall families.

The west end of the aisle is the work of Abbot Morwent, and is of the same date as his reconstructed west end of the nave—viz. 1421-1437.

The *west window* in this aisle was filled with glass by Hardman. It is a memorial to Wm. Viner Ellis of Minsterworth. Subject: Events in the life of King Lucius, who is said to have been the first Christian king in this land, and to have been buried in the Church of St. Mary de Lode.

The scrolls contain the monkish lines—

> Es merito celebris ex quo baptisma subisti.
> Lucius in tenebris prius idola qui coluisti.

The four figures represent Robert, Duke of Normandy; Thomas of Woodstock, 1397; Humphrey, 1447; William Frederick, 1534; all three of them Dukes of Gloucester.

The *first window* (or over the west door into cloisters), of which only two lights are open, is a memorial window to Thomas Churchus (1870). The window, which is by Clayton & Bell, is very pleasing in colour.

The *second window* is to the memory of Mr Price, who died in 1860. The glass is by Ward & Hughes.

The *third window* contains some old glass in the upper half, restored by Hardman. Much of the lower half is new.

The *fourth window* is a memorial window to Dr Hall, Master of Pembroke College, Oxford; died in 1843. The glass is by Clayton & Bell.

The *fifth window*, like the third, contains some old glass, restored by Hardman.

The *sixth window* is in memory of Bp. Hooper, second Bishop of this diocese, and the only bishop of the united sees of Gloucester and Worcester. The glass is by Clayton & Bell.

The *seventh window* is to the memory of Thomas Turner. The glass is by Clayton & Bell.

The *eighth window* is a memorial to members of the Darell family, as explained in the inscription in the base.

In the windows of the clerestory are to be seen some fragments of old glass. The windows, which are of three lights, contain portions of ornamental borders with quarry glazing, and some medallions, stars in the foliations, and borders of crowns. Mr Waller thinks it was "probable that all these windows were originally filled with glass of this kind, which is similar in general design to that in the upper tiers of the clerestory windows in the choir.

The tracery of the windows in the clerestory is ascribed to Abbot Morwent, who rebuilt the west front.

The **Monuments** in the north aisle are of no special interest. That to Bishop Warburton at the west end contains an epitaph that is worth reading. Next to it is an ungainly tomb, filling up an enormous wall space, with a depressing effect. Farther eastwards is the tomb by Flaxman to the memory of Mrs Morley, who died at sea in 1784.

The tomb to Alderman Machen, his wife, and family is interesting (1615), and is one of the few tombs that has not been removed from its original position.

The nave is lighted by rows of gas jets along the triforium or gallery, extending over the arches of the nave. The effect is good when the building requires to be lighted by artificial light, but the fumes and smoke from the gas have sadly discoloured the small columns and the arches in the triforium, and no doubt in time to come more serious mischief to the stonework will be developed. The fumes of the gas will also be fatal to the decorative pipes of the organ, and, with the assistance of the fumes from the radiators, will ruin any memorial brass that may be erected in the building.

Wires have been stretched across the nave to prevent the excessive echo from marring the effect of the music, but many curious echoes are to be heard. The mocking sounds that follow upon the sounds of the voice of a preacher, especially when the attendance is small, are very weird. They may be heard best from the last few rows of seats near the west end.

There are still to be found enthusiasts who would like to remove the screens from our cathedrals on the ground that they interfere with the utility and the beauty of the nave and the choir. But these well-meaning people quite overlook the fact that the beauty of the interior would be entirely marred by such a change. Firstly, the organ would have to be chopped into two and stowed away in the triforium, unless these enthusiasts would prefer to revert to an organ-gallery blocking up one of the transepts. Secondly, the stalls would have to be mutilated and rearranged. Certainly, the cathedral would resemble a parish church in some respects, but at a tremendous cost. There would be a vista, too, but the effect of the lofty choir would be lost entirely without the presence of the screen and the organ, and the nave would look more dwarfed in height. There is one more point, too, always forgotten by these enthusiasts—viz. this, that the building was not designed by Henry VIII. at the Dissolution as a parish church. He laid down quite clear and simple rules for the regulation of the cathedral foundation, and he intended the choir to serve, as it had served for the monks before, as the private chapel of those on his new foundation.

The **Choir Screen** was erected in 1820 by Dr Griffiths, to whose memory a tablet has been inserted in the northwest tower pier. Though this screen has its defects, it superseded one by Kent, erected in Bishop Benson's time

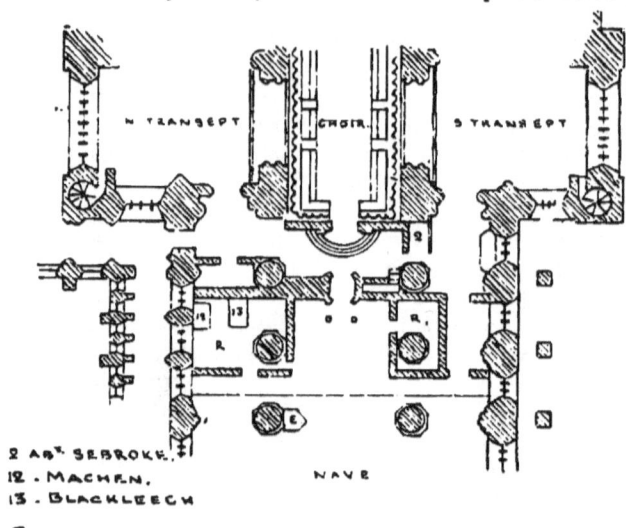

Drawn by F. S. Waller, F.R.I.B.A., from Brown Willis' Survey of Gloucester Cathedral (1727).

(1741), of which Bonner, who seems to have appreciated the stucco front applied by the same good bishop to the reredos in the Lady Chapel, says in his "Itinerary" (1796) that it combined the characteristics of the various orders of architecture without any of their good points.

To give an idea of the original screen arrangement, Mr Hope's description is here quoted:—

"The quire proper is under the Tower, a not unusual Benedictine arrangement. The original screens at the west end have unfortunately been destroyed, but from plans made by Browne Willis (*vide supra*, where Mr Waller's drawing of Browne Willis' plan, made in 1727, is given) and Carter, while some remains of them existed, the arrangement can be approximately recovered. I have advisedly used the plural word 'screens' because they were two in number. The first consisted of two stone walls—the one at the west end of the quire, against which the stalls were returned; the other west of it between the first pair of pillars. There was a central door, which was called the quire door. The western wall was broader than the other, and had in the thickness of its southern half an ascending stair to a loft or gallery above, which extended over the whole area between the two walls. This loft was called in Latin the *pulpitum*, and it must not, as it often has been, be confounded with the pulpit to preach from. It sometimes contained an altar, as apparently here at Gloucester, and on it stood a pair of organs. From it also on the principal feasts the Epistle was read and the Gospel solemnly sung at a great eagle desk. On either side of the *pulpitum* door was probably an altar.

"The double screen I have just described was built by Abbot Wigmore, who is recorded to have been buried in 1337, 'before the Salutation of the Blessed Mary in the entry of the quire on the south side,' which he himself constructed with the *pulpitum* on the same place *ut nunc cernitur* says the 'Chronicle,' and parts of it are worked up in the present screen. The north side of the quire entry, or perhaps the north quire door, was ornamented with images with tabernacles by Abbot Horton."

"The second screen, all traces of which have long disappeared, stood between the second pair of piers—*i.e.* a bay west of the *pulpitum*. It was a lofty stone wall, against which stood the altar of the holy cross, or rood-altar, as it was more commonly called, and upon it was a gallery called the rood-loft, from its containing the great rood and its attendant images. The rood usually stood on the parapet or front rail of the loft, but sometimes on a rood-beam crossing the church at some height above the loft. Such an arrangement seems to have existed at Gloucester, for in the sixth course from the top a new stone has been inserted in both pillars exactly on the line where the ends of the rood beam would be fitted into, or rested on corbels, in the pillars."

On either side of the rood altar the screen was pierced by a doorway for processions, and the altar itself was protected by a fence-screen a little farther west.

After showing how the counterpart of these arrangements existed at Durham (*vide Arch. Journ.* liv. pp. 77-119), and describing the Durham nave altar and rood, Mr Hope points out that at Gloucester, as at Durham, "the eastern of the two doorways between the nave and the cloister was shut off by the screen and reredos of a chapel adjoining it on the west. The monks could therefore freely pass through the cloister door without being interrupted by strangers. This eastern door was not only the ordinary entrance from the cloister, but through it passed the Sunday and other processions that included the circuit of the cloister and buildings opening out of it. The procession always returned into the church by the western cloister door, and, after making a station before the great rood, passed through the rood doors in single files, and entered the quire through the pulpitum or quire door."

In the chapel, on the north side (which was perhaps dedicated to St. Thomas the Martyr), was formerly, as shown in the plan by Brown Willis, the Blackleech monument, now in the south transept.

When the Benson screen was put up three Abbots were found interred in their robes, and another coffin with two skulls in it. This fact gave a possible clue to the identity of one of the Abbots. One probably was Abbot Gamage, and the two skulls probably belonged to his brother, Sir Nicholas Gamage, and his wife, who were buried near the Abbot.

The present **Organ** was built originally during 1663-1665 by Thomas Harris, the father of the celebrated Renatus or René Harris, and the cost was defrayed by public subscription, to which, however, the inhabitants of Gloucester contributed but little. The contract was for the sum of £400, exclusive of the sum for the building of the organ-loft, and the decoration of the pipes and the case. The gilding and painting was entrusted to Mr Campion in November 1664, and the work was finished in December 1666. This artist was celebrated as a painter of heraldic subjects, and the work done by him, chiefly on the large pipes of the Great, is particularly beautiful.

The shield, which has been removed from the west front of the case, was undoubtedly that of Charles II., and two of the large pipes facing the nave bear the letters C.R., with a crown over them. Other arms represented are those of James, Duke of York (king in 1685), and his first wife, Anne Hyde.

The organ was repaired by Bernhard Schmidt before 1683. It was formerly in the gallery of the south transept, over the stalls, but was placed on its present screen in 1820 by Dr Griffiths.

It was improved by Willis in 1847, and again in 1888-89, and further additions are contemplated. The case is of oak, and is a fine piece of Renaissance work. A good view of it can be obtained from the triforium, looking across from south-east to north-west.

The following is a specification (kindly sent by Mr A. H. Brewer, the organist of the cathedral), from which it will be seen that the instrument is worthy of the cathedral:—

GREAT ORGAN.
CC to A, 58 Notes.

1. Double Open Diapason . 16 ft.
2. Open Diapason, No. 1 . 8 ft.
3. Open Diapason, No. 2 * . 8 ft.
4. Claribel Flute . . 8 ft.
5. Flute Harmonique . . 4 ft.
6. Principal . . . 4 ft.
7. Twelfth . . . . 3 ft.
8. Fifteenth . . . 2 ft.
9. Mixture . . . .
10. Trombone . . . 16 ft.
11. Trumpet . . . 8 ft.
12. Clarion . . . . 4 ft.

SWELL ORGAN. †
CC to A, 58 Notes.

13. Double Open Diapason . 16 ft.
14. Open Diapason * . . 8 ft.
15. Vox Angelica . . . 8 ft.
16. Salcional . . . 8 ft.
17. Lieblich Gedact . . 8 ft.
18. Gemshorn . . . 4 ft.
19. Fifteenth . . . 2 ft.
20. Mixture . . . .
21. Contra Posaune ‡ . . 16 ft.
22. Hautboy . . . 8 ft.
23. Clarionet . . . 8 ft.
24. Cornopean . . . 8 ft.
25. Clarion . . . 4 ft.

CHOIR ORGAN.
CC to A, 58 Notes.

26. Stopped Diapason . . 8 ft.
27. Dulciana . . . 8 ft.
28. Flute . . . . 4 ft.
29. Clarionet . . . 8 ft.
30. Cor Anglais ‡ . . 8 ft.

SOLO ORGAN. §
CC to A, 58 Notes.

31. Flute . . . . 8 ft.
32. Clarionet . . . 8 ft.
33. Oboe Orchestral . . 8 ft.
34. Tuba Mirabilis . . 8 ft.

PEDAL ORGAN. ¶
CCC to F, 30 Notes.

35. Open Diapason . . 16 ft.
36. Bourdon . . . 16 ft.
37. Ophicleide ‡ . . . 16 ft.
38. Octave ‡ . . . 8 ft.

COUPLERS.

39. Choir to Pedals.
40. Great to Pedals.
41. Swell to Pedals.
42. Solo to Pedals.‡
43. Choir to Great.
44. Swell to Great.
45. Solo to Great.‡

* Stops so marked are by Harris, 1660.
† The swell organ was added by Willis in 1847.
‡ Stops so marked were added in 1898.
§ The whole of the solo organ was added by Willis in 1898.
¶ Up to within the last fifteen years there was but one stop on the pedal organ.

The **Choir**, of the beauty of which but little idea can be obtained from the nave, is entered by visitors, as a rule, from the north aisle of the choir. Its dimensions are—Length, 140 feet; breadth, 33 feet 7 inches; height, 86 feet; east window, 38 feet wide and 72 feet in height.

It dates back to the years 1337-1377—that is, the abbacies of Adam de Staunton and Thomas Horton, in whose time so much was done to alter the character of the building.

Looking upwards the visitor will note the beauty of the vaulting and the bosses placed at the intersection of the ribs. These bosses at the east end of the choir chiefly represent a choir of angels playing on various kinds of musical instruments, and a figure of Our Lord in the attitude of blessing. All the roof was originally probably painted and decorated, but the existing colour and gilding is recent work, having been done by Clayton & Bell. At first sight the groining of the roof looks most complicated, but, if analysed and dotted down on paper, it will be seen to be in reality a simple geometrical pattern. The bosses will repay careful examination with a glass.

Viewed from the door in the screen, the choir looks in very truth a piece of Perpendicular work, as the Norman substructure is then for the most part concealed. A closer examination, however, will prove that the Norman work is all there—that it has been veiled over with tracery from the floor level to the vaulting with open screen-work, fixed on to the Norman masonry, which was pared down to receive it. (*Vide* page 52.)

Professor Willis points out that "in all cathedrals . . . a screen, about the height of the present altar-screen, separated the choir from the side-aisles and transepts; but in this cathedral the screen is carried to the roof, and the result is a beautiful, if not unique choir. This screen of tracery, which formed the sides, was, below the clerestory, merely plastered on to the Norman wall; or the original Norman columns had been chipped down till they harmonised with the general design."

Professor Freeman, in writing of this casing work, said, "Paid for by the offerings at Edward II. shrine, . . . to that abnormal worship the abbey of Gloucester owed its present form. I am half inclined to put it the other way, and to make it a new count in the articles of deposition against the unworthy king that this misguided devotion has cost us the minster of Serlo in its perfect form, and hinders us from studying the contrast which we should otherwise have been able to mark between its eastern and its western limb."

We, however, have nothing to do with the question of the merits or demerits of Edward II. The beauty of the casing

Photochrom Co., Ltd., Photo.]
CHOIR, LOOKING EAST.

work compels our admiration. If we want to get an idea of what the choir would have been without the Perpendicular casing we must go to Norwich, and inspect the uncased work in the choir that is there, or else to Tewkesbury.*

There is nothing left to prove the original height of the choir, though much of the old stonework has been re-used in the clerestory windows, a practice, as before stated, common throughout the cathedral, the Norman piers and arch-mouldings having in many cases been turned into four-centred

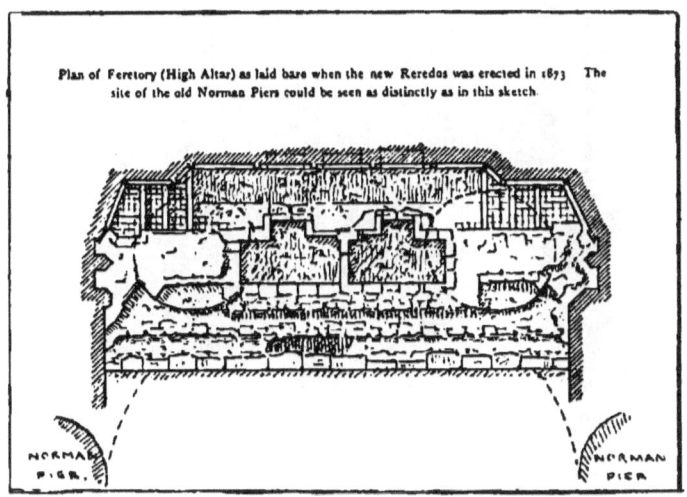

[From a Drawing by F. S. Waller, F.R.I.B.A.

arches, and Norman capitals into bases. The casing of the old Norman work with the new by Staunton and Horton is very ingeniously managed, and attention should be given to a feature resulting from the treatment of the ribs of the vaulting, which are very cleverly provided for in the centre of the tower arches. The ribs are apparently supported by a light arch thrown across the lower arches. Something of this sort was

---

* The abbey at Tewkesbury is a building which every visitor to Gloucester ought to make a point of seeing and studying. It was built on a similar plan, at the same time, and probably by some of the same builders who built Gloucester.

necessary, as the only alternative would have been to alter the springing of the vaulting-ribs. These light arches are very graceful and are best seen from the transepts or else from the

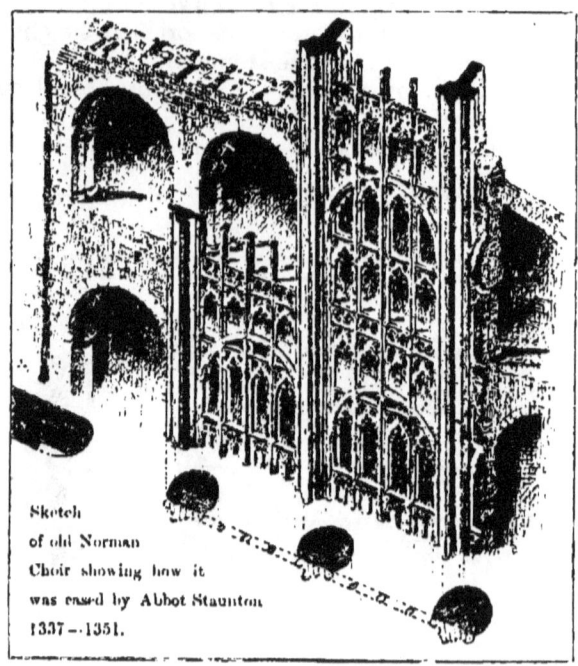

Sketch of old Norman Choir showing how it was cased by Abbot Staunton 1337–1351.

[From a Drawing by F. S. Waller, F.R.I.B.A.

triforium of the choir. Another feature worth noticing in the tower arches is the way that the two Norman columns are run into one capital at about the level of the arch.

Turning eastwards we next are struck by the loveliness of the **East Window** of the choir. It has a curious architectural effect, for it is actually 5 feet wider than the walls which seem to be its two boundaries. The architect took down the Norman east end, raised the roof, and has given us a window with lace-like tracery. Though it has suffered much mutilation, it has suffered but little from eager restorers, and it is possible to get some idea of its original splendour. It is larger than the East Window at York Minster, being 72 by 38 feet; York

Photochrom Co. Ltd., Photo.]

THE CHOIR, LOOKING WEST.

being but 78 by 33. Both are beautiful, and one wishes that windows of such beauty could be got now at the original price paid—£138—a large sum for those days, but a sum which, making allowance for the changed value of money, would represent about £2000 of our money.

In 1862 the stonework of the window was in a very unsafe condition, and about £1400 was spent on restoring it. At the same time, acting on Mr Winston's advice, the Dean and Chapter had the glass thoroughly cleaned and releaded.

Owing to Mr Winston's supervision the glass was not restored.

The window, which corresponds admirably with the casing of the choir and the clerestory windows, consists of fourteen lights altogether, six forming the centre, with four on either side. "It is worthy of remark that the tracery, heads, and cusps, as seen from the inside of this window, are not repeated on the outside, a plain transom only crossing the lights. This peculiarity is repeated also in the great west window, and in many other windows in the cathedral." (F. S. W.)

The window represents the coronation of the Virgin Mary, together with Christ, the Apostles, and various saints and kings. All the canopies, and nearly all the figures are composed of white glass enriched with yellow.

Mr Winston's description of the window will be found in the *Archæological Journal*, vol. xx.

The heraldic shields give a clue to the date of the window, and Mr Winston thinks that it may have been erected by Thomas, Lord Bradeston, to the memory of Sir Maurice Berkeley, who was killed at the siege of Calais, and to commemorate the glories of the campaign in France, which culminated with the Battle of Creçy. The date, therefore, of the original glass would be between 1347 and 1350.

Mr Winston further says that "It would be impossible to meet with white glass that could be more solid and silvery in effect. The red is beautifully varied, and is most luminous, even in its deepest parts, and the tone of the blue can hardly be surpassed." Of the general design, he says that although, "through the size and simplicity of its parts, it is calculated to produce a good effect at a distance; the figures are ill-drawn, ungraceful, and insipid. The shading, though sufficient, both in depth and quantity, if handled with skill, to have produced a due effect of relief—an effect which obviously has been aimed at—is so inartificially employed as to be useful only so far as it serves to impart tone and richness to the composition, and by contrast to increase its brilliancy."

The effect of the choir as a whole, when glazed with its original painted glass, must have been superb. We may be certain that the glass was the best that could be obtained, for the abbey was wealthy, and glass-painting was then a living art. Glass was made at Gloucester, as is shown by the glaziers being numbered among the trade companies and guilds of Gloucester, but there is nothing definite to be said as to the place of origin of the old glass in the cathedral.

Below is the **Reredos**, designed by Sir G. G. Scott, presented by the Treasurer of the Province. It consists of three principal compartments, in which are groups of figures (sculptured by Redfern) intended to represent the Birth, Burial, and Ascension of Christ. The smaller figures in the niches are Moses and David and St. Peter and St. Paul. Above are nine angels, bearing the various emblems of our Lord's Passion. This reredos was unveiled with much pomp and ceremony in 1873, and recently has been profusely gilded.

The commonplace and heavy-topped gas standards mar the effect, such as it is, of the ornate work of the reredos.

Of Abbot Horton's reredos, which was destroyed at the Reformation, only fragments remain. They have been very carefully preserved in the triforium, where an enclosure has been made by placing an old oak screen across one of the Chapels. In this museum most valuable remains have been stored, under Mr Waller's keeping, for many years.

Dean Chetwood, in 1710, erected a wooden reredos containing much good carving. Portions of this remain in the south-east chapel in the triforium of the choir, having been brought back from the parish church at Cheltenham, whither they had been removed in 1807.

Sir Robert Smirke in 1807 put up work which consisted chiefly of panelling, which was affixed to the easternmost wall of the feretory. This was removed in 1873.

When the present reredos was erected "the foundations of Abbot Horton's reredos were discovered, and an accurate plan was taken of the remains (*vide* illustration, p. 51). Provision had evidently been made by him for keeping relics or treasures here, and, in his time, the back screen, as we now see it, and the reredos, were united together at the top, and covered with

THE CHOIR IN 1806, FROM A DRAWING BY WILD.

heavy stone slabs, so as to make a perfectly secure feretory. Great care was taken during the progress of the present new work to preserve these remains, which can be still seen exactly as they were when first discovered. The foundations of the Norman piers removed by Horton were at the same time temporarily exposed to view." (F. S. W.)

The original "**High Altar** occupied the same site as the present one, and had behind its reredos a narrow space containing cupboards for the principal jewels, and, beneath the altar, two large recesses for the keeping of relics." (W. H. St. J. Hope.)

The **Stalls** (sixty in number), with all their graceful carving, and the misereres, with their grotesque ornamentation underneath, have in part had to be restored, while the sub-stalls are new, dating from Sir Gilbert Scott's restoration, which was finished in 1873.

An engraving (reproduced from Wild) will show what the choir was like formerly. The woodwork here shown has been utilised in making stalls and seats in the east end of the nave for the services that are held there on Sundays during a portion of the year.

In the **Presbytery**, or space between the reredos and the choir, there are some very splendid old tiles; many of them fragments only, but enough to indicate the original beauty of the pavement. From the evidence of the tiles themselves, they were laid down by Thomas Seabroke, R. Brygg (Brydges), J. Applebi, W. Farlei, Joh. Graft(on ?). Others dating back to the thirteenth century are also to be found—*e.g.* those to Richard the King of the Romans, who died in 1271.

Many tiles were transferred here from other parts of the cathedral early in the century by Mr Lysons, and this accounts for the presence of tiles of William Malvern, the last Abbot, and some others. The arms of the Brydges family: *Arg. on a cross sable, a leopard's face, or, differenced by a fir-cone gules*, should be noticed, as they seem clearly the same as those on the armour of the unknown knight in the South Transept.

Beautiful tiles, bearing the arms of Edward the Confessor and the Abbey, and many a crowned M. (for Maria) will be found. These latter will be seen in plenty in Great Malvern Priory, where they have been rescued from the pavement, and inserted in the outside wall of the back of the reredos.

One more tile should be noticed near the sedilia. The

words impressed in its surface are "*Croys Crist me spe de +,*" followed by *A ME* or *A MARIA*.

These tiles had a narrow escape in the last century, about the time when the nave was paved, when an offer was made to pave the presbytery with marble.

As part of the restoration programme, the re-paving of the choir was undertaken. New tiles, ostensibly copied from the old ones, but of a different size, with an excessive glaze, and very stiff in design and execution have been put down. It is hard to judge what the effect of the tiles would have been, as it has been quite killed by the white marble which has been mixed with them. The glaring white marble in the floor of the presbytery has been inlaid with biblical scenes outlined in lead. It is possible from the triforium to get a general idea of the crudeness and vulgarity of the pavement, which is so composed and arranged that time—the softener of all things—can never make it look appreciably better.

On the south side of the high altar are four **Sedilia**. These have been very much restored, and the niches and canopies filled with figures, by Redfern, representing Abbot Edric, Bishop Wulstan, also Abbots Aldred, Serlo, Foliot, Thokey, Wygmore, Horton, Froucester, Morwent, Seabroke, and Hanley. The general effect is good, but marred by the hideous gas standards.

Over the canopies are three angels playing on a tambour and trumpets. The rod and entwined ribbon with T. O. are supposed to refer to Thomas Osborne, Sheriff of Gloucester 1512-1522, and Mayor in 1526.

Monuments in the Choir.—On the north side of the presbytery, near the steps to the high altar, is a monument—long supposed to be a cenotaph—to King Osric. The tomb was opened to satisfy inquisitive desecrators some few years ago, and it was conclusively proved that someone had been buried inside.

On the wall is the inscription : *Osricus Rex* (*primus fundator*) *hui* (*Monasterii* 681). From Leland, to whom is due the part of the inscription in brackets, we learn that " Osric, Founder of Gloucester Abbey, first laye in St. Petronell's Chappell, thence removed with our Lady Chappell, and thence removed of late dayes, and layd under a fayre tombe of stone on the north syde of the high aulter. At the foote of the tombe is thus written in a wall "—*ut supra*.

This "fayre tombe" was erected in "late dayes" *i.e.* in the time of Abbot Parker, whose arms are in the spandrels of the canopy, dated (1514 to 1539), and Leland must have seen the tomb in all the freshness of its beauty.

The Norman piers, which are cut away to receive the tomb, are decorated as to their capitals with the device of Richard II. *i.e.* the white hart chained and gorged, with a ducal coronet. Formerly these devices were painted on the stone, but in 1737 they were blazoned on thin metal by the Heraldic College, and put in position. From the occurrence of the device in this place it was formerly held that the body of Edward II. was drawn by stages from Berkeley Castle to the abbey.

The other coats-of-arms are those of the abbey (they are blazoned as they should be now—azure, a sword in pale, hilted, pommelled, and crowned, or, surmounted by two keys in saltire of the last), and of Osric as King of Northumbria. Osric is represented as crowned and sceptred (clad in tunic, laced mantle, and a fur hood or collar) bearing the model of a church in his left hand.

The next tomb westwards is, as Leland says, that of "King Edward of Cærnarvon (who) lyeth under a fayre tombe, in an arch at the head of King Osric tombe."

The **Tomb of Edward II.** was erected by Edward III., and though it awakens our recollection of a feeble-minded king, and his barbarously brutal murder, it also compels our admiration at the beauty of the work. It has been restored, renovated or re-edified, but in spite of that, appeals to us from the wealth of very highly ornate tabernacle work, the richness, and at the same time the lightness and elegance of the whole. The details too are well worth careful examination. It may be, judging from the expression of the face, that there has been some attempt at portraiture, but repair and restoration have practically made it impossible to settle what would otherwise be an interesting question. The superb canopy has suffered much at the hands of restorers—*e.g.* in 1737, 1789, 1798, and in 1876.

The alabaster figure is possibly the earliest of its kind in England.

The tomb was opened in October 1855 by Dr Jeune, Canon in residence, to satisfy the curious who doubted whether the king had been buried under his tomb. Close by is the chantry tomb of William Malverne (or Parker), Abbot of the Abbey

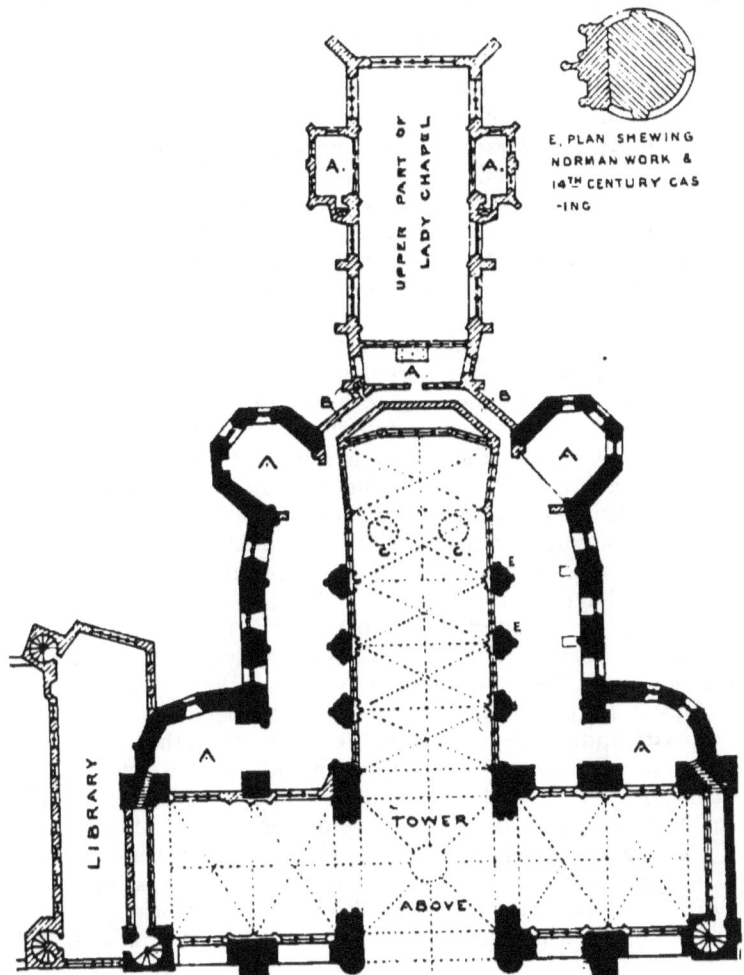

PLAN OF TRIFORIUM OF THE CHOIR.
[From a Drawing by F. S. Waller, F.R.I.B.A.

from 1515 up to the time of the Dissolution. It was erected in his lifetime, but he is buried elsewhere.

On the stone screen the carving of the vine and the grapes will be found worthy of notice. The alabaster figure has been terribly defaced, but the chasuble and the mitre can be seen, and the broken staff. Around the base of the tomb are panels. Both sides are alike, containing the Abbot's own arms, and the emblems of the Crucifixion. At the foot is a cross composed of a tree with its branches growing into the shape of a cross. There is a very good tile on the floor with the arms of the Abbey, and some specimens of tiles, with a very fine greenish glaze upon them. Some of the large $7\frac{1}{2}$-in. tiles with the stag —the Abbot's own arms—are particularly good.

On the south side of the choir the bracket tomb or monument, so called from the effigy being placed on a corbel or projecting bracket, should be noted. It is said by some to be Aldred's, by others to be Serlo's monument. The date of the monument is later than either in point of time. The mutilated effigy bears a model of a church in his left hand, and this points to its being the monument to a founder. It is more than probable that it is to the memory of Abbot Henry Foliot, in whose time (1228-1243) the church was re-dedicated.

The monument, which is Perpendicular and Early English, has been much battered, but it is exceedingly graceful and of an unusual type.

Leland, who visited the Abbey in 1539 or 1540, wrote as follows:—"Serlo, Abbot of Gloucester, lyeth under a fayre marble tombe, on the south side of the Presbytery."

Glass in the Choir.—Mention has been made above of the east window, and it remains to notice the others.

In the clerestory on the north side the windows have been restored by Clayton & Bell. They are best seen from the triforium, but are given here as being part of the choir. Following the example of the lights in the east window, these clerestory windows have alternately red and blue backgrounds. Portions of old glass remain in the heads of the windows.

Beginning with the windows west to east the *first* contains:

   (1) St. Zacharias. (2) St. Elizabeth. (3) St. John Baptist. (4) St. Gabriel.

The *second* contains:

   (1) St. Anna. (2) St. Mary. (3) St. Joseph. (4) St. Gabriel.

The *third* contains:

    (1) St. Peter. (2) St. John. (3) St. James (Major). (This light is out of its place.) (4) St. Andrew.

The *fourth* contains:

    (1) St. Philip. (2) St. Bartholomew. (3) St. Simon. (4) St. Jude.

The clerestory windows on the south side are filled with stamped quarries with central medallions and coloured borders, made after the model of remains of ancient painted glass.

The choir also contains a peculiarity in its six-light west window. This was rendered necessary by the difference in height of the nave as compared with that of the choir. The choir vaulting is about twenty feet higher than that of the nave. The glass at present in the window consists chiefly of patchwork, arranged by Hardman from pieces collected and saved at different times from other windows in the cathedral. It represents a figure of our Lord, with angels on either side. Below are angels playing on musical instruments.

It is customary to credit the Reformation or the Civil War with most church desecration and destruction, but this window was ruthlessly destroyed by an order of the Chapter in 1679, nearly thirty years after the Civil War was ended, and nearly 140 years after the dissolution of the monastery. The order ran as follows: "That a certain scandalous picture of ye Holy Trinity being in ye west window of ye Quire of ye said church, should be removed, and other glass put into ye place." The glass of the window was actually broken up by one of the prebendaries (Fowler by name) with his own hands and feet. His action, considering his views, was incomprehensible; but he was made Bishop of the diocese, after Bishop Frampton was deprived of his see. Beneath the west window is an inscription (restored) in the panelling of the stone work:

| Hoc quod | digestum | specularis | opusque | politum | Tullii haec |
| Ex onere | Seabroke | | | abbate | jubente. |

These two Latin verses record that "this work (viz. the tower) which you see built and adorned, was done by the labour of Tully, at the command of Abbot Seabroke."

Robert Tully was a monk of Gloucester, and was Bishop of St. David's, where he died in 1482. There is a brassless slab to his memory there, but the best monument is the tower that was built by him here in Gloucester.

After passing through the iron gate into the last bay of the south aisle, the tomb of Abbot Seabrook or Seabroke will be seen on the left, inside a stone screen, through which formerly was a doorway giving access to the organ loft. The alabaster effigy represents the Abbot in his alb, stole, tunic, dalmatic, chasuble, amice, and mitre, with his pastoral staff on his right side. The chapel has been partially restored. Traces of colour are to be seen in the reredos and the roof over it.

Abbot Seabroke's pastoral staff was discovered in 1741 in his coffin while the tomb was being removed. After changing hands many times it was acquired finally by the Antiquarian Society of Newcastle-on-Tyne.

In the west end of the Seabroke Chapel, against the first pier of the nave, is a mural monument, rather florid in style, to Francis Baber, 1669.

Close to the Seabroke Chapel, on one of the piers supporting the tower, is a bracket with traces of very beautiful blue colour. The canopy above—much mutilated—shows traces of red, blue, and gold.

Almost opposite to this, but nearer to the iron gate, is a recessed tomb to a knight in mixed armour of mail and plate, and by his side his lady, with kirtle, mantle, and flowing hair. Both wear SS collars, and this helps to give the age of the monument, by narrowing the date down to a year not earlier than 1399. The SS collars also tend to disprove that the monument is to Humphrey de Bohun, Earl of Hereford, and his countess, seeing that he died in 1361. On the knight's belt is a badge, very much worn down, which has been attributed to the Brydges family. Mr Lysons thought it to be the tomb of Sir John Brydges who fought at Agincourt, and died in 1437, but the mail tippet is not found later than 1418. The tomb may commemorate Sir Thomas Brydges, who died in 1407, and this would agree better with the date given above.

The transepts and ambulatory of the choir are entered, as a rule, by the iron gateway in the south aisle of the nave.

South Transept.—This transept, like that on the north, underwent a complete transformation in the fourteenth century, under Abbot Wygmore (1329-1337). In spite of the transformation, the Norman design can easily be traced both in the inside and the outside of the transept. The walls have been ornamented with open panelled work, consisting of mullions and transoms, with very rich tracery and foiled headings. The method of the casing is best seen from the triforium, where the original Norman masonry can be closely inspected. The panel work, in spite of its date, has the appearance of being considerably later, and some have thought the work to have been executed after Wygmore's time.

Professor Willis thinks that the Perpendicular style, which elsewhere—*e.g.* in the north transept and the choir—is completely developed, may have had its origin in this south transept. In any case, the work is of the greatest architectural interest, and deserves careful study. "Looking at the very early character of the clustered shafts and the mouldings of this transept in conjunction with the vertical lines with which they are associated, one might think (excepting Thokey's south aisle, the Edward II. monument, and some few examples in the triforium of the choir) that Decorated work had never fairly taken root in Gloucester." (F. S. W.)

The south transept, which was also called St. Andrew's Aisle, is 47 feet long, 35 feet broad, and 86 feet in height. The vaulting is lierne vaulting, with short ribs, which connect the main ribs together. There are no bosses in the roof. With an opera-glass it is possible to note the clever joining of the masonry.

On the north side of the south transept, between the tower piers, is an interesting chapel, with a wooden screen—date about 1510. The panelling inside, as also that on the back of the choir-stalls here exposed to view, is covered with monograms of S and B alternately, all surmounted with crowns.

The chapel is said to have been dedicated by John Browne (or Newton), who was Abbot from 1510-1514, to his patron saint, St. John the Baptist, the initials being the same.

On the step in this chapel is a slab with a mutilated cross incised in it and remains of an inscription upon a scroll. It is now almost illegible and crumbling fast away, but it was

"Kyrie eleison anime
Fratris Johis Lyon."

E

This Johannis Lyon was the monk who made the reredos in this chapel. There are traces of two reredoses here, both of which show traces of colour. Older stonework has been used to make the newer reredos, and has been merely reversed.

The tiles here are of interest, and there are also some outside, both at the east and at the west end of the chapel screen, well worthy of attention. They are chiefly odd tiles, similar to those in the choir, with the name of Farley, others with oak leaves, others with fleur-de-lys, others with lions rampant.

At the west end of the chapel outside is a highly lacquered brass of the usual type, in memory of Judge Sumner, 1885.

Just before turning into the south transept a stone on the floor will be seen, close to the angle of the wall made by the transept and the south aisle, with the inscription: "Here lyeth under this marbell ston Robart Leigh, organist and Maister of the Choristers of this Cathedral Church. He dyed the 6th of January 1589" (?). No record of him survives.

On the south wall are two doorways. One, which is blocked up, is in the south-east corner, and is surmounted by a double-bodied monster, resembling an ape. The other doorway is usually pointed out to visitors as the "Pilgrim's door."

Whether this door was that in general use for pilgrims or not is an open question. It was for a long time blocked up and has only a makeshift door in it at the present time. Carter, writing in 1807, says: "The arch of the opening, in its head, has four turns concentred by a flower. Above the head is an ogee architrave rising from small columns, which columns bend forward on each hand, forming open arms or fences on each side of the steps to the doorway. On these arms recline statues (angels) acting as guardians to the doorway. Their attitudes are well conceived and pleasingly varied." The sculpture is extremely graceful and pleasing, the expression of the faces particularly charming. The drapery, too, is arranged in a masterly manner.

The door was thought by some to have been used to admit pilgrims to the shrine of Edward II., but others, arguing from the angels upon it, have taken it to be the door by which penitents could retire after making their confession. Perhaps the most reasonable explanation is that it was a door communicating with a vestry or checker for the sacrist, but there are no traces underground outside the south wall of any stone foundation for such building.

On the east side of the transept will be noted the restored **Chapel of St. Andrew.** The paintings on the wall were executed in 1866-67 in spirit fresco by Mr Gambier Parry for Thomas Marling, Esq., in memory of his wife, who died in 1863.

The reredos contains a central figure of the Saviour between St. Andrew and St. Peter, with eight figures of smaller size— viz. Job, Solomon, Moses, David, Isaiah, Jeremiah, Ezekiel, Daniel. The remainder of the figures are intended to represent a choir of angels.

The tiles in the chapel are very bright and gaudy, contrasting unfavourably with the older tiles elsewhere in the building. The arrangement of the tiles on the risers of the steps is very monotonous and unpleasing. Plain stone steps would have been far less obtrusive.

At one time a charge of sixpence was made for the privilege of inspecting the interior of this chapel, but nowadays it is kept closed. For many years it was used as a vestry for the lay clerks. The windows contain glass (by Hardman) dealing with events in the life of St. Andrew.

In the east window, over St. Andrew's Chapel in the south transept, is to be seen some of the best glass now to be found in the cathedral, dating back to about 1330. It consists in the head of a white scroll-work of vine leaves, etc., on a fine ruby-coloured ground, and below plain quarries with very simple borders. These have been releaded by Hardman.

On either side of the chapel there are tabernacles. That on the south side contains some very fine carving, and with one boss quite complete. The colour, judging from the traces remaining, must have been very charming.

On the north side of the chapel is the **'Prentice's Bracket**. In shape it resembles a mason's square supporting an apprentice. Underneath it, as a supporter, is the master mason. The work was probably intended to carry an image with a pair of lights, and also to serve as a memorial of the workmen.

The Elizabethan monument erected in memory of Richard Pates, Esq., founder of the Grammar School at Cheltenham, is a poor example of its date, 1588. The next monument was originally in the north choir chapel of the nave (*vide* Brown

Willis' plan, p. 44), and commemorates Alderman Blackleech, in cavalier costume, and his wife. The date of the tomb is 1639. Other and later memorials are on the walls, but they are of no special interest.

There is an interesting tablet to Canon Evan Evans, D.D. (Master of Pembroke College, Oxford), who died in 1891. The memorial consists of a bronze tablet, bordered by a frame of marble inlaid with other marbles. The bronze at the top is inlaid with shell of an iridescent colour. The general effect is good, but silver hardly seems suited for inlaying in a building lighted by gas. The tablet was designed by Mr H. Wilson. The west window is Perpendicular, and is filled with glass in memory of Mr T. G. Parry.

The south window in this transept has been filled with glass (by Hardman), at the expense of Thomas Marling, Esq.

The slabs on the floor have been moved from the positions they formerly occupied, and have suffered by the change. A large slate-coloured stone, which used to be in front of the Blackleech monument is now placed much nearer the entrance to the crypt. It is broken in two and is covered up by matting.

Another stone slab has traces of a mill wheel. The inscription on it used to tell that " Here lyeth buried the body of John Long, Millard and Milwright, who departed this life the 16th day of April 1596."

A blue-coloured slab, which originally had a fine brass inlaid canopy has been converted to the use of a Minor Canon named Deane—1755.

The large buttress which passes through the St. Andrew Chapel upwards through the triforium, to support the south-east pier of the tower, used formerly to bear upon it a monument to Bishop Benson, which is now in the south triforium.

The double doorway which gives access to the choir aisle, and to the crypt, seems to be the type of several other doorways of later date in the building, as, for instance, in the north transept, and also in doorways in the Deanery and cloisters.

The **Crypt*** is one of five English eastern crypts, founded before 1085, the others being those at Canterbury, Winchester, Rochester, and Worcester, and extends underneath the whole

* The Crypt is described here because it is, as a rule, entered from the eastern door in the south transept.

THE INTERIOR

of the choir, the ambulatories or aisles of the choir, and the five chapels belonging thereto.

In passing downstairs to the crypt or under-church, an inscription over the door of the chapel on the right refers to the enormous quantity of bones which had accumulated in the crypt, and thus obtained for it the name of " The Bone House." These bones had been brought in from the south precincts

S. B. Bolas & Co., Photo.]
S.E. CHAPEL IN THE CRYPT.

outside, all of which had been formerly a burying-ground, and in 1851 were removed to the south-west chapel of the crypt, and later buried in a large grave on the north side of the cathedral.

The crypt consists of an apse, three small apsidal chapels —*i.e.* a N.E., an E., and a S.E. chapel, and also two chapels underneath the eastern chapels of the north and south transepts.

"The outer walls of the crypt are about 10 feet thick, and the aisle floor is on an average 8 feet below the level of the soil on the outside of the building. The centre part is divided by two rows of small columns, irregularly placed, from which spring arches carrying the floor of the choir above; the bases and capitals of these small capitals are much out of level from west to east, and from north to south, and in design they vary greatly as to their capitals, abaci, and bases. All of these are strikingly different to the half columns with cushion capitals attached to the outer walls, on which rest the ribs they mutually carry. So different, indeed, are they as to make it questionable if by far the larger portion of these columns does not belong to our earlier church."

"Great alterations have from time to time been made in the crypt. The large semi-circular columns against the walls, though of great antiquity, are not parts of the original structure, but are casings built round, and enclosing the former smaller piers, and the ribs springing from their capitals are built *under*, with a view to support the vaulting." (F. S. W.)

This strengthening work was rendered necessary owing to earthquake shocks which occurred, and possibly from the fact that the originally defective foundations on the south side of the crypt caused a slight settlement.

It may be noted here that the masons' marks found in the triforium on the Norman work are also found in the crypt on the later strengthening work, and not upon the Early Norman work. This fact has been considered to prove that the crypt was built by Aldred.

The first chapel—*i.e.* that below St. Andrew's Chapel—contains a double piscina with a shelf in good preservation. There are remains of hinge-posts (two sets), and the holes for the movable bar with which the doors could be fastened.

The second chapel—*i.e.* that underneath St. Philip's Chapel—contains an arcade of five plain arches with ornament above. There is also a double piscina with shelf in good preservation, and a large altar-step, 6 feet 2 inches by 4 feet.

The third or eastern chapel, which is under the vestibule leading into the Lady Chapel, contains portions of the building which have had to be replaced by recent work, and some fragments of tombstones, one bearing the inscription *Gilbertus*.

The fourth chapel, which is underneath Abbot Boteler's

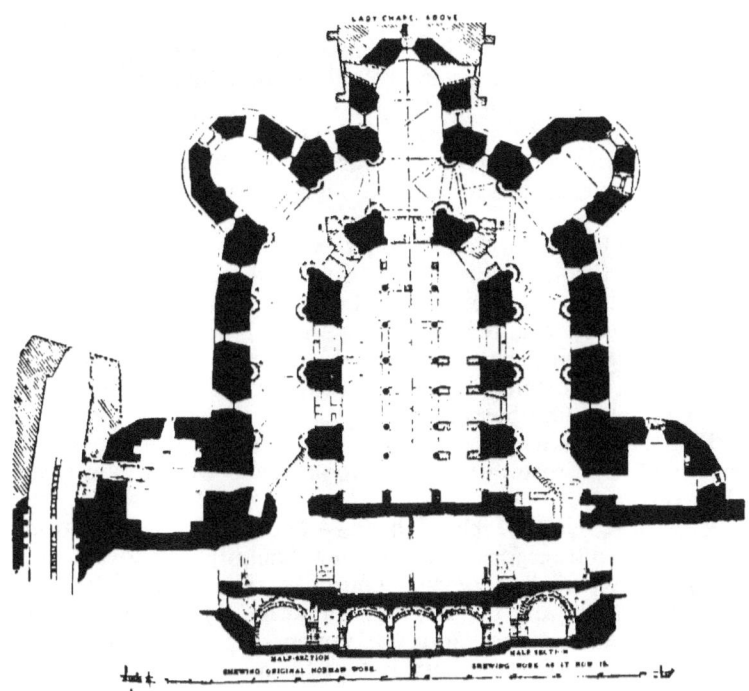

PLAN OF THE CRYPT.

[From a Drawing by F. S. Waller, F.R.I.B.A.

The dark tint on the walls represents the Early Norman Crypt.

The second period of Norman work is shown by the double lines round the small shafts at A A, which denote masonry erected some time after, to carry the ribs which strengthen the vaulting.

The parts sectionised were for the most part built in the fourteenth and fifteenth centuries to carry the walls above—notably s s, as foundations for the choir piers.

Chapel, also contains fragments, some of them very beautiful specimens of stonework. There is also a slab, upon which is to be read the words, *Orate pro aia fris Johis.* This slab was formerly in the south transept, and was (according to Mr Haine's transcription of the slab made thirty years ago) to the memory of John Lempster, who lived in Abbot Froucester's time.

A slab inscribed I STAUNT, which used to be in the cloisters at the entrance to the chapter-house, is also in the crypt. This John de Staunton was akin to Abbot Staunton, who was buried in 1351.

The fifth chapel, which is underneath St. Paul's Chapel, was the chapel through which the Abbot had access to the crypt from the Abbot's cloister. The easternmost portion has some very good vaulting and decoration of the thirteenth century, and contains a very mutilated piscina. The groining of the roof is, unfortunately, falling away by degrees. There are traces of some fine bosses.

The crypt was cleared, drained, and concreted in the course of the restoration that took place during the years 1853-1863.

Ambulatories of the Choir.—These aisles have nothing uncommon in their form or arrangement below, but above occurs the great peculiarity of this church. The side aisles and eastern chapels are, in fact, including the crypt, three storeys high, and all vaulted, and the upper range of chapels surrounding the choir is perhaps not to be met with in any other church in Europe.

Near the entrance to the **S. Ambulatory of the Choir** a tomb and brass to the memory of Rev. John Kempthorn, B.D. (1838) will be found on the right, near the side entrance into St. Andrew's Chapel.

Close to it, upon the floor, is a modern brass, by Messrs Heaton, Butter & Bayne, to the memory of Rev. H. Haines, M.A., who for twenty-three years was second master in the cathedral school. He died in 1872. His book on the Cathedral, which he knew so thoroughly and loved so well, is one of the best guide-books to the building, but, unfortunately, no new edition has been issued since 1884.

Some of the piers in the south ambulatory of the choir will be found to show traces of colour decoration in certain lights,

As a whole they retain more Norman work, unaltered, than perhaps any other portion of the building.

Near to the Kempthorn monument is the memorial window to Canon Harvey and his wife, who both died in the year 1889. The glass is by Kempe.

The second window, also by Kempe, is a memorial to the Rev. H. Law, who was Dean from 1862-1884. The figure drawing in this light will attract notice.

The third window, glass by Kempe, is a memorial to the Rev. Sir J. H. Culme Seymour, Bart., who was Canon of Gloucester for fifty-one years, and died in 1880.

The Triforium of the Choir is, perhaps, the finest triforium in existence, and is worthy of special examination. " It occupies the space over the ground floors of the aisles or ambulatory of the choir, and originally extended of a like width round the east end of the Norman Church, but at the time when the fourteenth-century work of the present choir was executed, the whole of the east end of the old Norman choir, with the corresponding part of the triforium, was removed in order to make room for the existing large window, the small east chapel being allowed to remain." (F. S. W.) The original shape of this part of the building will be more clearly seen by reference to the chapel (D), indicated by dotted lines on the plan, and to the extreme east chapel of the crypt. As the means of entrance to this east chapel of the triforium was now gone, the narrow gallery usually called the "Whispering Gallery" was made, and carried by segmental arches, marked BB, from the south-east to the east chapel, and from the east chapel to that on the north-east. The external appearance of the Whispering Gallery is shown on page 75. The casual observer frequently takes it to be a piece of Norman work, but it is in reality the material of Norman builders very skilfully re-used.

The triforium is reached by the staircases in the western turrets of the two transepts and by arcaded passages passing under the great windows of the transepts. Excellent views across the transepts are thence to be obtained. Still better views can be got from the corner of the triforium (near the painting of the Last Judgment), both across the organ to the north side of the nave, down the south aisle, and also across the choir,

The first chapel in the triforium contains two brackets with rich canopies, and there is a very well preserved double piscina. Ball-flowers in two rows will be found in the mouldings of the east window. Remains of two canopies in the jambs of the windows are also to be traced.

The massive Norman piers should be carefully studied, as the way in which the later casing work has been applied can be more easily seen in the triforium than elsewhere.

The picture on the west side of this part of the triforium was discovered in 1718, against the then eastern end of the nave, underneath the panelled wainscot at the back of the seats occupied by the clergy when the nave was used for service.

During the last few years it has lost much of its colour; it is painted *in tempera* on a kind of gesso ground laid on a wooden planking nearly an inch thick. From the size of it—viz. 9 feet $10\frac{1}{2}$ inches by 7 feet $7\frac{1}{4}$ inches—it was formerly thought to have formed part of the reredos.

Portions of the original frame remain, and they show traces of gilding upon them. The picture has been varnished to preserve it, and, although hung in a wretched situation for light, it is worth more than passing attention. Christ is represented in the centre, throned on a rainbow, attended by angels, and having a globe and a cross below Him. His mantle is red, with a jewelled border. On either side of His head are emblems—on the left a lily, emblematic of mercy; and on the right a sword, emblematic of justice. The lily inclines towards the righteous, and the sword points towards the wicked. Below on the left are six apostles, but above these is an angel holding a T cross and the crown of thorns. To balance this, on the right is an angel with a whipping-post, a scourge, and a spear. Over these figures are scrolls, one on the left inscribed "Come, O you blessed . . .", and on the right, "Go, O you cursed . . ." In the centre, under the globe, is an angel holding an open book, "The boke of côsciens"—*i.e.* the book of conscience. On either side are angels blowing upon trumpets, from which extend scrolls inscribed, "Aryse, you dede. Come to your judgement"; and below this the Resurrection is depicted. An angel (in the centre) is scaring away a horned demon from the soul borne up by the angel. On the right the wicked are being carried off by fiends; on the left the righteous are being led away by angels bearing crosses.

THE INTERIOR

In the left-hand bottom corner are angels and inscriptions. "Before man lyfe and death. In all thy workes remêbre thy

S. B. Bolas & Co., Photo.]
SOUTH-EAST VIEW OF CATHEDRAL, SHOWING WHISPERING GALLERY.

last, and never wilt thou offend." In the top corner on the left is represented the New Jerusalem. The architecture is classic in character.

St. Peter and an angel are standing close to a gate into which the righteous are entering. A choir of angels with musical instruments are above.

In the bottom corner on the right the mouth of hell is represented, into which the lost are being thrust by attendant demons. There is a grim figure inside a globe, possibly intended for the Prince of this world, seizing a soul by the

Photochrom Co. Ltd., Photo.]
TRIFORIUM OF THE CHOIR, LOOKING EAST.

hair. At the bottom are other fiends helping to torture the unhappy lost.

Mr G. Scharf, jun., in *Archæologia*, vol. xxxvi., says that the picture is English, and is of great importance. He thinks it was painted during the latter years of the reign of Henry VIII. or during that of Edward VI., and points out that it is an epitome of the famous altar-piece at Dantzig, painted in 1467. It is remarkable that in this picture the Virgin and St. John the Baptist, who are usually associated in pictures with the Saviour, are altogether omitted.

The second, or south-eastern chapel, contains many interesting remains of coloured tiles, old carving, some being linenfold panels. There are also some finely-carved pilasters, which once formed part of the Queen Anne reredos, put up by Dean Chetwood about 1710. This reredos was taken down in 1807, and was for many years in the old church at Cheltenham. When, however, the church at Cheltenham fell into the hands of the restorer, parts of the carved work were brought back to Gloucester.

Passing towards the Whispering Gallery, the flying buttresses inserted to support the walls of the clerestory, which were weakened by the insertion of the great east window of the choir, 1347-1350, should be noticed.

The **Whispering Gallery**, to which the ordinary visitor pays more attention than anything else in the building, has remarkable acoustic properties. A whisper (the lower in tone the better) can be easily and distinctly heard at the other end of the gallery, and to this peculiarity the following lines, by Maurice Wheeler (head-master of the King's School, 1684-1712) have reference :

> " Doubt not but God, who sits on high,
> Thy secret prayers can hear,
> When a dead wall thus cunningly
> Conveys soft whispers to the ear."

Lord Bacon seems to have thought over the subject of the gallery, and his remarks are here quoted : " I suppose there is some vault, or hollow, or isle behind the wall, and some passage to it, towards the farther end of that wall against which you speak, so as the voice of him that speaketh slideth along the wall, and then entereth at some passage, and communicateth with the air of the hollow, for it is preserved somewhat by the plain wall : but that is too weak to give a sound audible till it has communicated with the back air."

The gallery is a passage of Norman work, very much altered and re-used. It is 74 feet long, 3 feet wide, 6½ feet high, and is carried on segmental arches from the east end of the south triforium to the west wall of the Lady Chapel, and from thence in the same way to the north triforium. On page 75 will be seen the appearance of the little bridge thus made.

In passing through the gallery access is obtained to a chapel on the right, which is immediately over the entrance vestibule to the Lady Chapel. From this chapel a very good general view of the Lady Chapel can be obtained. The bosses in the roof show to greater advantage, and it is possible to see more of the colour that remains on the walls.

This chapel is smaller than the others in the triforium, and was reduced in size when the west end of the Lady Chapel was built. The altar slab is original Norman work, and has three or four ✣ inscribed in it.

S. B. Bolas & Co., Photo.]
SOUTH AMBULATORY OF THE CHOIR.

The pieces of old glass formerly in this chapel have disappeared, and modern ornamental quarries and medallions, by Hardman, have taken their place.

The fourth chapel has nothing of note in it beyond the window tracery.

The fifth chapel, or the one nearest to the north transept, contains a double piscina, in very good preservation.

The triforium contains a few monuments, chiefly those that

have been removed from the nave. Bishop Benson's monument was formerly on the face of the buttress that passes through St. Andrew's Chapel.

The triforium seems a better resting-place than the crypt for monuments which are rejected from the nave and elsewhere. It is to be hoped that in the years to come no restorer will lay hold upon the monuments in the Lady Chapel and transepts, and consign them to oblivion in the neighbouring garden of the deanery. This was done in Dean Law's time, and may in part be the reason why the cathedral is so poor in specimens of monuments of the Queen Anne period.

The **South-East Chapel**, which is dedicated to St. Philip, contains some interesting features. The arches are of a distinctly "pointed" character, and there are remains of the two bases of pillars which supported the stone altar slab.

This chapel was restored in memory of Sir C. W. Codrington, Bart., M.P., who died in 1864. Various incidents in the life of St. Philip have been painted on the vaulting by Burlison & Grylls, but the paintings have suffered somewhat from damp. The window, which is by Clayton & Bell, is of no special interest, and represents saints, principally British, and striking incidents in the life of each in the panel under each of the figures.

Near the piscina, at the base of a pier, will be found some dog-tooth moulding. This is repeated on the other side of the chapel, but not on the corresponding pier.

Before entering the Lady Chapel, a Perpendicular arch will be noticed, with two eye-shaped openings in the spandrels. The openings are well carved on their bevelled edges. The arch is of later date than the front of the chapel, and seems to have been necessary to support the triforium above. Nothing like it exists on the other side. There is an old cope-chest in this Ambulatory.

The **Lady Chapel**.—This beautiful chapel, which was built between the years 1457-1499 by the Abbots Richard Hanley and William Farley, stands on the site of a smaller building, dating back to 1224, and erected by Ralph de Wylington and Olympias, his wife, the architect of the work being Elias or Helias the Sacrist, a monk of the Gloucester monastery. As Mr Bazeley points out ("Records," vol. iii.

pt. 1, p. 14), "The only architectural evidences of its former existence are two Early English windows in the crypt, in the central eastern chapel."

Mr Waller thinks that this Early English Lady Chapel was "probably not a new building, but simply an alteration of the old east apsidal chapels on each floor to suit the 'Early English' times, just as the fourteenth-century men afterwards recased the cathedral. The inserted windows of this date in the crypt seem to confirm this view."

On the site of this chapel must have stood the chapel and altar (or at any rate the altar) dedicated to St. Petronilla, as Ralph and Olympias gave rentals to provide lights to burn thereat during mass for ever.

The vestibule or entrance to the Lady Chapel is a beautiful piece of work, and is another instance of the genius of the builders shown in making use of existing work. Special interest attaches to this chapel as a whole, as it was the last addition to the fabric by the monks before the Dissolution.

Firstly the walls of the vestible should be noticed: the lower portions of the west wall are parts of the old Norman apsidal chapel, and are pierced by the opening for the door and by two perpendicular windows; and the west end of the chapel is contracted in breadth, as it is also in height, so as to minimise the loss of light to the great window of the choir. The shape of the chapel will be easily understood from the plan (p. 61).

The lierne vaulting of the vestibule is very delicate (the ribs, it will be noted, are run differently in the four quarters of the roof), and the pendants form a cross. These latter, at the present time, look new, but they have only been freed from the whitewash that was thick upon them. One pendant has been renewed at the end. Over the vestibule is the small chapel which is entered from the Whispering Gallery (*vide* page 77).

The open tracery of the west end over the supporting arch is particularly graceful, especially the way in which the open lights are arranged in the central portion. The Lady Chapel is 91 feet 6 inches long, 25 feet 6 inches high, and 46 feet 6 inches high, and consists of four compartments or bays, which, as the wall of the chapel is so low, are chiefly composed of fine tracery and glass. All the wall below the windows is arcaded with foiled arches, with quatrefoils above them. The wall between the windows is panelled with delicate tracery like that in the windows, and in its three chic tiers contains brackets for figures, with richly-carved canopies overhead. Many of these canopies (like the walls) show traces of colour.

Photochrom Co. Ltd., Photo.]
THE LADY CHAPEL.

Vaulting shafts of great beauty support one of the grandest Perpendicular roofs that has ever been made. Each boss in the roof is worth minute inspection, and since the restoration (1896) it is possible to see the bosses in practically the same condition as they were when they left the masons' hands in the fifteenth century. With three exceptions they are all representations of foliage, and it would be a hard task to arrange them in order of merit.

It has been said above that the chapel is cruciform. The arms of the cross are represented by the two side chapels, like diminutive transepts on the north and south sides, with oratories above them, to which access is given by small staircases in the angles of the wall. Both these side chapels contain some exquisite fan-tracery vaulting, which is supported upon flying arches, fashioned in imitation of the graceful flying arches in the choir.

On the north side the chapel contains a full-length effigy of Bishop Goldsborough (who died in 1604) robed in his white rochet, black chimero, with lawn sleeves, scarf, ruff, and skull-cap.

The east window in this chapel is in memory of Lieut. Arthur John Lawford (1885), and is dedicated to St. Martin.

The chapel above has a vaulted roof with bosses of foliage, and there are small portions of ancient glass.

Bishop Nicholson's tomb, which was formerly in the south chapel, where it blocked up the east window, is at present in pieces in this upper chapel. It is to be re-erected in another place.

There are some interesting scribblings on the walls of this chapel. On the shelf for books is a representation of a Cromwellian soldier with a dog, apparently in pursuit of a deer. There are also scribblings with devices, dating to 1630-1634. One love-sick swain described an equilateral triangle with a ✚ rising from the vertex, and then inscribed the initials of his *fiancée* and also his own.

In the south chapel there are scribbles, dating back to 1588 and 1604. Both of these chapels have shelves for books, but it is probable that one was for a small choir and the other for an organ.

The **South Chapel** contains an altar tomb to Thomas Fitzwilliams, who died 1579, and there is a wooden tablet, painted with an inscription to tell that it was repaired in 1648.

A window has been put up in memory of S. Sebastian Wesley, a former organist of the cathedral, who died in 1876.

This chapel is one of the largest in the kingdom, and is said, at the time of the Dissolution, to have been one of the richest. A great part of it is said to have been gilded and gloriously ornamented. Traces of the colour can be seen in the mouldings of the panellings and in the carving upon the walls.

S. B. Bolas & Co., Photo.]
WEST END OF LADY CHAPEL.

The **Reredos**, judging from the traces that are left, must have been a gorgeous sight, and literally a blaze of colour. Appliqué work has been lavishly employed in its decoration.

Anyone who is privileged to examine it very closely will note the writing on the stonework, which has been laid bare in the niches by the ruthless removal of the figures. At present what the present Dean, in his article on the Great Abbeys of the Severn Lands, calls its "pathetic scarred beauty," is temporarily veiled by a very modern screen. The reredos, though a ruin, has a charm all its own, and it is better to leave it frankly as it is now than to partly hide it. There are some, no doubt, who would restore it, but it is to be hoped that funds will not be forthcoming. Restoration has effectually marred the beauty of the pavement of the choir, and given us a flashy reredos there, of which the less said the better; but every one with a particle of feeling must feel that restoration and decoration of the Lady Chapel reredos would be a crime.

Bishop Benson covered the reredos with stucco, and put up a huge gold sun in front of it. Portions of this are now at Minsterworth. An engraving of it may be seen in Bonnor's "Perspective Itinerary," published in 1796, and this plate also shows the long rows of pews removed from the choir by the same bishop.

The sedilia are very fine, and worthy of careful inspection.

The **East Window** consists of nine lights, and has been terribly mutilated, partly by fanatics, partly owing to lack of care within the last century. In design the window resembles the windows on the north and south sides of the chapel. It was erected in Abbot Farley's time (1472-1479), and possibly by a Thomas Compton, seeing that in the quatrefoiled circles in the heads of the lower lights there are rebuses—a comb with TŌ, and CŌ with a TON (for Compton), as well as two intertwining initials. Much of the glass seems to have been put in after removal from other windows in the cathedral, and this makes the deciphering of this window no easy undertaking.

The tiles in the Lady Chapel are of great interest, and one cannot help regretting their gradual deterioration under the feet, occasionally the hobnailed feet of visitors, and the slower but surer destruction by the accumulations of grit under the matting on the floor. They may be best examined by turning up the matting near the Clent tablet on the south wall.

On a pattern made up of sixteen tiles, four times repeated

THE INTERIOR

can be read, "*Ave Maria gra' ple' Dus tecum*" i.e. "*gratia plena Dominus tecum.*" On others similarly designed, "*Domine Jhu (Jesu) miserere.*" On others, "*Ave Maria gra' ple'*" and "*Dne Jhu miserere.*" These tiles in square sets of sixteen and four respectively were placed alternately, and separated by plain dark bricks. On others again will be found "*Orate pro Aïa Iohis Hertlond (pro anima Johannis).*" Some too seem to have been transferred from Llanthony Priory to the south chapel. They are inscribed, "*Timetib' deŭ nihil deest,*" i.e. "*Timentibus deum nihil deest.*" There are others in the chapel, "*Letabor in mia—et sethera,*" and "*Deo Gracias.*"

The monument to Sir John Powell (1713) on the north wall is not beautiful, though a good specimen of its time. It is impossible not to regret that it was ever allowed to be erected in the chapel. Powell was a judge of King's Bench, and is here represented in his gown, hood, mantle, and coif.

Other monuments are those to Eliz: Williams, 1622 (the figure is raised on one elbow); to Margaret Clent, 1623, with a touching epitaph. On the floor, near the Williams monument is a small brass, concealed by matting, to Charles Sutton, an infant seven days old. The brass contains two Latin lines modelled on the lines of Ovid's "Tristia," and run:

> "Parve, nec invideo, sine me, puer, ibis ad astra,
> Parve, nec invideas, laetus ad astra sequar."

Many of the slabs on the floor will repay perusal, most of them being well cut and fairly well preserved. In Brown Willis' "Survey of Gloucester" will be found a full record of all the tombstones which in his time (1727) were in this chapel, but have since been removed or re-used.

Turning to the right on leaving the Lady Chapel, the north-east chapel, which is called **Abbot Boteler's Chapel**, is the next in order. It dates from 1437-1450. The reredos should be closely examined, as it retains many of its original features —viz. statuettes, traces of painting on the shields above, and a very good piscina.

The tiles in the floor are in many cases excellent specimens, especially those with fish upon them. It seems a pity that these tiles should be doomed to disappear under the nails of sight-seers, who as a rule look at nothing but the effigy of

Robert, Duke of Normandy, and go away satisfied when they have proved for themselves that the effigy is of wood.

The effigy has had a curious history. As Leland says, "Rob^{tus} Curthoise, sonne to William the Conquerour, lyeth in the middle of the Presbitery. There is on his tombe an image of wood paynted, made long since his death." As to the date there is great uncertainty, and it would seem that the figure and the chest upon which it lies are not of the same date. Sir W. V. Guise in "Records of Gloucester Cathedral," vol. i., part 1, p. 101 (now out of print), says, "I am disposed to assign to the effigy a date not very remote from the period at which the duke lived. The hauberk of chain-mail and the long surcote ceased to be worn after the thirteenth century," and on p. 100, "The mortuary chest on which the figure rests is probably not older than the fifteenth century..." Around the chest are a series of shields bearing coats-of-arms, ten in number, nine of which were originally intended to commemorate the nine worthies of the world. On the dexter side: 1. Hector. 2. Julius Cæsar. 3. David. 4. King Arthur. On the sinister side: 5. Edward the Confessor. 6. Alexander the Great. 7. Judas Maccabæus. 8. Charlemagne. 9. (at the south end) Godfrey of Bouillon. 10. (at the north end) The arms of France and England, quarterly. The blazoning of 10 proves the chest to be later than the time of Henry IV.

The oak figure was broken into several pieces in the civil wars of Charles I., but was bought by Sir Humphrey Tracey of Stanway, who had it repaired, and presented it to the Cathedral.

Leland says that the duke "lyeth in the middle of the Presbitery." The inscription in the chapter-house says "Hic jacet Robertus Curtus." The plain pavement in the choir is said to mark the site of the grave in the choir, but it is open to question whether there would be space for interment between the tiling and the upper side of the vaulting of the crypt. It is to be hoped that at some future time the effigy may be moved back to its place in the Presbytery.

The next chapel—*i.e.* the north-west chapel, is dedicated to St. Paul, and is entered by a doorway, with the initials T. C. over it, in the spandrels. T. C. may stand for Thomas Compton.

The windows in the north ambulatory of the choir are as follow:—

The window next to Boteler's Chapel is a memorial

TOMB OF ROBERT CURTHOSE.

Photochrom Co. Ltd., Photo.

erected by the dean and chapter to Mrs Tinling. The glass was designed by the late J. D. Sedding, Esq., and was executed by Kempe.

Opposite to the tomb of Edward II. is a memorial window, also by Kempe, to the late Lieut.-General Sir Joseph Thackwell and his wife.

The third window is a memorial to Alfred George Price, who died in 1880, and it represents the four great builders of the church—viz. 1. King Osric. 2. Abbot Serlo. 3. Abbot Wygmore. 4. Abbot Seabroke.

Opposite this door in the north-east corner is a doorway—Perpendicular in style—with interesting cresting and carving, giving access to the vestries and the choir practising-room.

In this, as in the other chapels, the groined edge of the Norman vaulting is carried down the piers.

The reredos in this chapel was more perfect, in point of good repair, than any other in the building, and the chapel was repaired by the late Earl of Ellenborough in 1870, figures by Redfern representing St. Peter, St. Paul, and St. Luke being inserted in the niches.

At the back of the reredos are windows (by Burlison & Grylls) representing in the side-lights angels with instruments of music, and in the centre Our Lord in majesty with angels bearing crowns and branches of palm.

On the south side of the chapel is a brass tablet in memory of Dean Law, who was Dean from 1862-1884. The combination of copper, brass, and gun-metal is to be regretted, as the workmanship is above the average, and the design is good. It is a mistake to paint heraldic devices on brass.

Close by the door leading into the north transept will be seen the stone reading-desk, from which it is said addresses were given to the many pilgrims who came to the shrine of the unfortunate Edward II.

The **North Transept.**—This transept, like that on the south, consists of Norman work, which was cased over by Abbot Horton during the last years of his abbacy (1368-1373) with fine Perpendicular panelling, cleverly engrafted into the original wall. It will be noticed that the work is, though Early Perpendicular, much more fully developed than that in the south transept. Angular mouldings of great beauty are used in the place of round mouldings; the mullions run right up to the roof, which again is much richer than that in the south transept. The vaulting of the north transept somewhat resembles in character the fan-tracery of the cloisters, the junction of the main and transverse vaults being rounded rather than angular, and the smaller ribs springing from between the larger ones a little *above* the union with the capitals of the supporting shafts. This transept is 8 feet lower than that on the south side. It is 2 feet shorter, and 1 foot less in width.

On the north side, " under the north window, is a beautiful

Photochrom Co. Ltd., Photo.
NORTH AMBULATORY OF THE CHOIR, LOOKING EAST.

piece of Early English work (c. 1240), which is supposed to have been a **Reliquary**."

It is constructed in three divisions, that in the middle being a doorway. Foiled openings enrich all the arches, and the carving of the foliage is very beautiful. Purbeck marble shafts are placed at the angles, and corbel heads at the spring of the arches, except at the north-east corner, where a stone shield, with arms of Abbot Parker, are substituted. Much of the figure-work on the outside has been mutilated. In the inside the roof is simply groined, with bosses, one of which in the central division is most beautifully wrought; and there are, too,

THE INTERIOR

small heads which, fortunately, seem to have escaped notice altogether, and are almost perfect. In Bonnor's "Perspective

S. B. Bolas & Co., Photo.]
NORTH AMBULATORY OF THE CHOIR, LOOKING WEST.

Itinerary," 1796, it is described as punishment cells. Mr Bazeley thinks it was part of the Early English Lady Chapel, built in 1227, which, being thought worthy of preservation, was taken down and re-erected here when the present Lady Chapel was built.

Opposite to the reliquary is a **Chapel** between the tower piers, said to be dedicated to **St. Anthony.**

DOOR FROM NORTH TRANSEPT INTO NORTH AMBULATORY OF THE CHOIR.

[From a Photograph by Miss Dawson of Cardiff

The wood panelling on the back of the stalls of the choir shows traces of painting, representing the soul of a woman at the mouth of a hell or purgatory, praying to St. Anthony, who is depicted with his pig and a bell. Other figures are there, but they are beyond recognition. This chapel is used as the

Dean's vestry, and contains some old panelling, re-used, and two old strong-boxes.

Beneath the niche, near the door leading into the North Ambulatory of the Choir, is an inscription, which is now barely legible (even with an opera-glass)—*Orate pro aia (Magistri Johannis) Schelton*; at least so Brown Willis read it in 1727. On the floor of this transept are some slabs, now brassless, under which have been buried men of note in the early days of the history of the building. One mutilated slab, 7 feet 1 inch by 3 feet 4 inches, has an inscription, of which some only is now legible in the border. From Brown Willis' "Survey of the Cathedral," 1727, it can be seen that it is to Robert Stanford.

The inscription was—

Hic jacet Robertus Stanford quondam serviens hujus monasterii et specialis ac munificus benefactor ejusdem qui obiit vicesimo secundo . . .

A brass to Wm. Lisle, 1723, has been inserted.

Abbots Horton, Boyfield, Froucester were all buried in this transept, but beyond crediting the stone that shows a trace of a mitre to Froucester, it is a mere matter of speculation to distinguish between the others. The stone next but one to it contains the matrix of a fine cross. The north window was filled in 1874 with glass by Hardman in memory of Sir Michael Edward Hicks-Beach, Bart., M.P., and his wife. The subjects are episodes in the life of St. Paul.

Under the west window of this transept is a curious painted monument to John Bower and his wife (1615). They had "nyne sones and seaven daughters," who are represented in perspective on the wooden panel against the wall. The tomb is barely characteristic of its date. On the top is an inscription —*Memento mori*; also, *Vayne, vanytie, witnesse Soloman, all is but vayne.*

The colour on the tomb has suffered from whitewashing at various times, and the tomb has been scorched by the heat generated by the warming apparatus in the corner, to the detriment of the painted panel.

The west window of this transept was put up in 1894, in memory of Wm. Philip Price, M.P. This window is too full of detail, and the canopy work is overdone. The glass is by Kempe.

The east window contains some old glass, releaded by Clayton & Bell.

CHAPTER IV

THE PRECINCTS AND MONASTIC BUILDINGS

WITHIN the area once contained by the boundary walls of the Abbey (for which see the plan on p. 103) there are remains of four of the original **Gateways**. The finest of these is that which leads into St. Mary's Square, and the best view of it is obtained from the steps of the memorial to Bishop Hooper. It is a very typical specimen of Early English work. "It has a gate porch entered by a wide but low pointed arch, with an inner arch where the doors were hung. The gatehall thus formed also had doors towards the court, and in its south wall are two recesses. The upper storey has, towards the street, an arcade of four arches, and the outer pair have each a trefoiled niche or panel in the back. The other two arches are of larger size and are both pierced with two interesting square-headed lights, also of the thirteenth century, with dividing mullions. In the gable, within a large triangular panel, is a niche of three arches, originally carried by detached shafts, but these are now broken away." (Hope.)

Tradition has it that Bonner watched the burning of Bishop Hooper from the window over this gateway.

The "inner gate gave access to the inner court, known of late years as Miller's Green, where the bakehouse, boulting-house, brew-house, stable, mill, and such-like offices were placed. It was also the way to the later Abbot's lodging. The existing gateway is of the fourteenth century, and has a single passage, in the west side of which is a blocked doorway. The passage is covered by a lierne vault."

"The gateway on the south side, towards the city, has been almost entirely destroyed, and only a fragment of the west side remains. It was known as 'King Edward's' gate, from its having been built by Edward I. It was afterwards restored and beautified by Abbot Malverne, *alias* Parker, 1514-1539. The remaining turret of the gate, on the west side towards the church, is probably part of Parker's work." (Hope.)

On the south side of what is left of this gateway are the arms of King Osric, as King of Northumbria. The stone bearing these arms was dug up some seventy years ago and was placed in its present position.

In College Court, a narrow turning leading from the north side of Westgate Street into the close, is a small gateway, consisting of a flattened archway, with canopied niches at the sides. This is also supposed to have been built by Abbot Parker. The upper portion, which was destroyed, has been converted into very commonplace offices.

In the north-west corner of the precincts was the **Vineyard**. The vineyards of Gloucestershire used formerly to be famous. William of Malmesbury, in the twelfth century, writes: "This county (Gloucestershire) is planted thicker with vineyards than any other in England, more plentiful in crops, and more pleasant in flavour. For the wines do not offend the mouth with sharpness, since they do not yield to the French (wines) in sweetness." The Gloucestershire vineyards survived as late as 1701. The curious terraces or step-markings on the Cotswolds in various places, locally called "litchets" or "lyches," are by some supposed to have been portions of the sites of these vineyards.

"The **Dorter** (says Mr Hope) and its *basement* are now destroyed, and their plan and extent are at present uncertain: but owing to its south wall having been partly that of the chapter-house also, one small fragment has been preserved which . . . helps to fix the position of the dorter. This fragment, which may be seen on the north-east corner of the chapter-house, is the jamb of one of the windows built between 1303 and 1313, and its date is clearly shown by the little ball-flowers round the capital of the shaft." The dorter then may be assumed to have occupied the space between the chapter-house and the end of the east alley of the cloister.

The **Refectory** (or Frater), "which was begun in 1246, on the site of the Norman one destroyed to make room for it, was a great hall over 130 feet long and nearly 40 feet wide. It was reached by a broad flight of steps, beginning in the cloister and passing up through the frater door. The steps did not open directly into the frater, but ended in a vestibule screened off from the rest of the hall, and covered by a loft or gallery. Into this vestibule would also open the service doors from the kitchen and buttery. . . . The west end and nearly all the north side have been pulled down to the ground, but the south wall, being common to the cloister, remains up to the height of its window sills. The east end is also standing to the same height. . . . Much of the stonework of the east and south walls is reddened by the fire that destroyed the frater in 1540."

ST. MARY'S GATE.   KING EDWARD'S GATE.
Drawn by F. S. Waller, F.R.I.B.A.

The **Little Cloisters** consist of an irregular quadrangle, with sides of varying length. The garth wall is a good specimen of Perpendicular work. There are five openings on each side. In the times of the Great Rebellion the little cloisters were partly unroofed. The western alley is part of an interesting fifteenth-century house which is built over it, and the south alley has a lean-to roof.

The other two alleys, which are now unroofed, were formerly covered by part of a large building which was built

THE PRECINCTS AND MONASTIC BUILDINGS 97

over them, and called Babylon. All traces of Babylon have now disappeared.

In the north wall of the cloister three stone coffins have been built in with the masonry. Mr Hope thinks it quite possible that this small garth was used as the herbarium or herb garden.

"On the west side of the little cloister, and partly over-riding it, is a medieval house of several dates, from the thirteenth century to the suppression, and later. Owing, however, to modern partitions and fittings,

COLLEGE GATEWAY. GATEWAY INTO PALACE YARD.
Drawn by F. S. Waller, F.R.I.B.A.

and repeated alterations, it is somewhat difficult to trace its architectural history. The oldest part of it consists of a vaulted undercroft of Early English work extending north and south beneath the western part of the house. It consists of three bays, of which two now form the kitchen of the house, and the third or northernmost is walled off to form a passage outside. More work of the same period adjoins this on the west, including a good doorway with moulded head. This doorway was clearly, as now, an external one. The undercroft stops short about twelve feet from the frater wall (or wide enough to leave a cart-way), and there is nothing to shew that it extended further east. Looking at its position so near the great cellar, the kitchen, and other offices, it is very probable that the original upper floor was the cellarer's checker, or counting-house, and the undercroft a place for stores."

Close by, to the north-east, are to be seen six graceful arches of Early English work. These are a portion of the remains of the "infirmary" or "farmery," which was "deemed superfluous" at the suppression, and for the most part pulled down.

"The chapel was destroyed and the great hall unroofed and partly demolished, but its west end and six arches of the arcade escaped, the

Photochrom Co. Ltd., Photo.]
REMAINS OF THE INFIRMARY.

latter probably because, as at Canterbury, the south aisle had been previously cut up into sets of chambers. All these remains are of admirable early thirteenth-century work, and it is much to be regretted that in clearing away the old houses in 1860 it should have been found necessary to also remove a curious vaulted lobby and other remains on the east side of the little cloister. The main entrance was originally in the west end of the hall, where part of the doorway still remains, and was probably covered by a pentise or porch with a door (still remaining) from the infirmary cloister, so that there was a continuous covered way from the farmery to the church." (Hope.)

"The **Library** is an interesting room of the fourteenth century, retaining much of its original open roof. The north side has eleven windows, each of two square-headed lights and perfectly plain, which lighted the bays or studies. The large end windows are Late Perpendicular, each of seven lights with a transom. There are other alterations, such as the beautiful wooden corbels from which the roof springs, which are probably contemporary with the work of the cloister, when the western stair to the library was built and the room altered. None of the old fittings now remain, but there can be no doubt that this was the library." (Hope.)

The library of the monastery, judging by the list given by Leland, must have been of considerable value and of no little interest. A list of the books it contained is given in "Records of Gloucester Cathedral," vol. i. pp. 145-6.

The books were at the time of the dissolution of the monastery confiscated to the Crown,

MEDIÆVAL HOUSE.
From a Drawing by E. J. Burrow.

and the cathedral was apparently without a library till the time of Bishop Godfrey Godman, who was consecrated in 1624. Writing to his clergy in 1629, he says: "I am to lett yow understand that I have lately erected a Librarie in Glouc^{r.} for the use of all our brethren throughout my Dioces, as likewise for the use of Gent. and Strangers, such as are students. I conceave it will not onely be most usefull, but likewise a great ornament to Citie and Dioces." He goes on to ask the clergy to give either "a booke or ye price of a booke," and tells them not to "inquire what bookes we have or what are wanting, ffor if we have double we can exchange them." Thoroughly business-like and considerate, the bishop also says: "If any man's weake estate and povertie be such that he can neither give booke, nor price of booke, yet in manners and courtisie (seeing his diocesan require it), I doe expect that he should excuse himselfe, and I will take the least excuse, without any further inquirie, as lovingly as if he had given the greatest gift." He was tender-hearted to his curates, for he says, "Neither doe I write this to Curates or Lecturers, unlesse themselves please to bestow; only I do expect from them that they acquaint the parsons and vicars, and returne their answers unto mee."

This, then, was the beginning of the Cathedral library. Later, in 1648, after troublous times in Gloucester, when even the cathedral itself was in danger, Thomas Pury, jun., Esq., with the help of Mr Sheppard, Captain Hemming, and others, made this library at considerable expense, and, as Sir Robert Atkyns quaintly observed, "encouraged literature to assist reason, in the midst of times deluded with imaginary inspiration."

In 1658, after the "late Cathedrall Church of Gloucester" had been settled upon the Maior and Burgesses for publique and religious uses, the Common Council vested and settled the library on the Maior and Burgesses, and their successors *for ever.*" The Restoration, however, in 1660, made still another change, and the library then became the property of the Dean and Chapter.

Sir Matthew Hale was a liberal benefactor to the library.

Owing to the damp in the Chapter-House, which for many years had to serve as the library, the books, in 1743, were removed into the south ambulatory of the choir. This was done by order of the Dean and Chapter, but the Chapter-House was apparently in use as a library in 1796, when Bonnor was making the drawings for his "Perspective Itinerary." In 1827 new and lower cases for the books were fitted, and the Chapter-House was used up to 1857 as the Cathedral library. Since that time the old monastic library has been restored to its original use.

The **Chapter-House** is entered from the east alley of the cloister through a Norman archway of very good work, enriched with zig-zag ornament.

Originally consisting of three bays of Norman work, it probably, like the chapter-houses at Norwich, Reading, and Durham, terminated in a semi-circular apse. The present east end is of Late Perpendicular work, and makes a fourth bay. Judging from the method in which the new work was joined on to the old in the fifteenth century, it would seem as if the builders intended to remodel the whole building. The vaulting of the later part is well groined, and the window is good. The roof of the three Norman bays is a lofty barrel vault supported by three slightly-pointed arches springing from the capitals of the columns, which are curiously set back, and separate the bays.

Norman arcading of twelve arches—*i.e.* four to each bay, runs along the three westernmost bays on the north and south walls, and in the arcading are inscriptions restored from the description given by Leland. Below the arcading "may be traced the line of the stone bench on which the monks sat in chapter." (Hope.) The floor has been considerably lowered in modern times. The tiling is modern, having been copied by Minton from the old work, both as to subject and arrangement.

"The west end is arranged in the usual Benedictine fashion, with a central door, flanked originally by two large unglazed window openings, with three large windows above. . . . Only one of the windows flanking the doorway can now be seen, the other having been partly destroyed and covered by Perpendicular panelling when the new library stair was built in the south-west corner of the room." (Hope.)

"At the south-west corner of the chapter-house is a large winding stone staircase, with a stone handrail worked in the newel, and also in the side wall." (F. S. W.)

The lower part of this west wall shows distinct traces of fire, which the upper part does not. This seems to confirm the idea that when the fire of 1102 broke out and destroyed so much, it burned down the cloister and the temporary roof of the chapter-house, both of which were probably of wood.

Walter de Lacy was (Hart. i. 73) buried in the chapter-house with great pomp in 1085, and the room must have been ready or nearly ready for use in that year. As Fosbroke

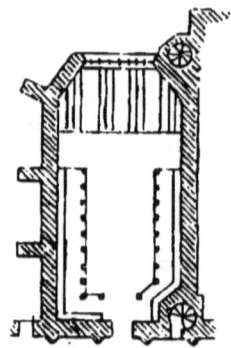

Plan of the Chapter-House, as shown —A.D. 1727—in Willis' "Survey of Cathedrals." A good general idea of the fittings formerly in the Chapter-House may be seen in Bonnor's work, published in 1799, but on his plan they occupy the two bays eastward, instead of west, as here delineated. They appear to have been excellent Renaissance work.

CHAPTER-HOUSE.

naïvely says of the distinguished dead who are buried here, "They could not have been buried in this room before it existed."

In Leland's time the names were painted on the walls near their gravestones in Black Letter. As he says, "These inscriptions be written on the walles of the chapter-house in the cloyster of Gloucester: *Hic jacet Rogerus, Comes de Hereford; Ricds Strongbowe, filius Gilberti, Comitis de Pembroke; Gualterus de Lacy; Philipus de Foye Miles; Bernardus de Novo Mercatu; Paganus de Cadurcis; Adam de Cadurcis; Robertus Curtus.*

Of the names given by Leland it may be noted that Roger, Earl of Hereford, Bernard de Newmarch ("Novo Mercatu"), and Walter de Lacy, were all contemporaries of the Conqueror, and "much about his person." They, therefore, when money was being collected for the abbey buildings, subscribed, adding some reservation as to the places in which they wished to be interred.

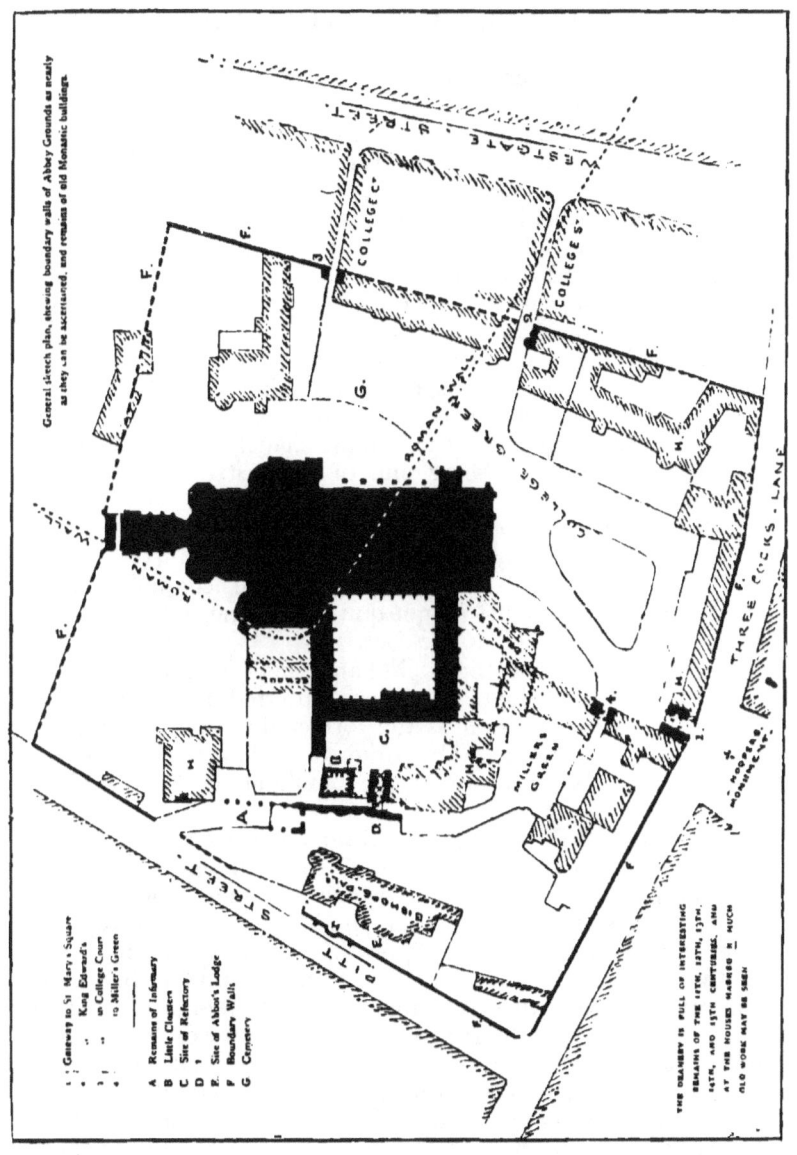

In spite of the wires stretched across the building, there is a remarkable echo.

The **Cloisters** are entered from the church by a door near the organ screen in the north aisle of the nave. They were begun by Abbot Horton (1351-1377), who built as far as the door of the chapter-house, and finished by Abbot Froucester, 1381-1412. It will be noticed how the mouldings, the tracery of the windows, and the character of the work generally differ. It is perhaps no exaggeration to say that "the cloisters are some of the finest and most perfect in the kingdom. They form a quadrangle, and are divided into ten compartments in each walk. The vaulting is of the kind known as fan-tracery, and is considered to have originated in Gloucester. It is found also at Peterborough, at Ely, and in the chapel of King's College, Cambridge, the latter being one of the last examples of the method.

"The outer walls are substantially of Norman date, but now overlaid and refaced by Perpendicular panelling." (Hope.)

Though the cloisters are quadrangular, the length (147 feet) of each of the four walks is not quite the same, but the width is 12½ feet and the height 18½ feet.

East Alley.—On the right-hand side in this walk will be noticed a new door. This was inserted in 1874 in the wall in the same position as the former door into the monks' *locutorium* or parlour. The original wide opening of the doorway may be seen under the moulding of the panelling on the wall.

The passage to which the glazed door gives access "is chiefly of early Norman date, and was originally of the same length as the width of the transept against which it is built. It was entered from the cloister by a wide arch, and has a wall arcade on each side of fifteen arches on the north, but only eleven on the south, the space between the transept pilaster-buttresses admitting no more than that number. The roof is a perfectly plain barrel vault without ribs. In the south-west corner is a hollowed bracket, or cresset stone as it was called, in which a wick floating in tallow was kept to light the passage."

"It having become necessary in the fourteenth century to enlarge the vestry and library over the passage, its east end was taken down and the passage extended to double its former length. At the same time a vice, or circular stair, was built at the N.E.

angle to give access to the library. To prevent, however, the new stair from encroaching too much on the apse of the chapter-house, the addition to the passage was deflected a little to the south instead of being carried on in a straight line. The vault of the added part is a simple barrel like the Early Norman work. The use of this passage was twofold. First, it was the place where talking was allowed at such times as it was forbidden in the cloister. Hence its name of *locutorium*, or, in English, the parlour. Secondly, it was the way for the monks to go to their cemetery. When the present cloister was built the original use of the parlour seems to have passed away, and in the new works the arch of entrance was blocked up and covered by the new panelling. Since this also cut off all access from the cloister to the library stair, a new stair was built at the west end directly accessible from the cloister. For want of room this had to be intruded into the south-west corner of the chapter-house." (Hope.)

Above the passage are two floors, one being the vestry, entered from the north-east chapel of the choir, and the upper one, the library, now restored to its original monastic use after many vicissitudes.

This east alley "was used as a passage between the church and the farmery, and the later Abbot's lodging; out of it also opened the parlour, chapter-house, and dorter door." (Hope.)

"In the third bay from the church the southern half is pierced with a door below the transom. On the cloister side of the southern half of the second bay, and of the northern half of the fourth bay, there was, in each case, built out a little cupboard or closet, now destroyed. These may have been used for keeping books in. This alley has no bench against the walls." (Hope.)

Opposite the fifth bay in this alley is the doorway, containing some good Norman work, slightly restored, leading into the chapter-house.

"The construction of the outer walls of the east walk is peculiar as to the arrangement of the buttresses and the projecting shelf of stone connected with the transoms of the windows, which was evidently meant as a protection from the weather for the lower half of the windows, at that time not glazed." (F. S. W.)

The first window in this east alley or walk, beginning at the south corner, nearest to the door into the north aisle, is one of four lights, by Hardman, to the memory of Rev. H. Burrup, a missionary, who died in Africa in 1862.

The second window (also by Hardman) is a memorial to Rev. John Plumptre, who was Dean from 1808-1825.

The third window (also by Hardman) is a memorial to Archdeacon Timbrill.

The fourth window (by Hardman) is a memorial to the Hon. and Very Rev. Edward Rice, who was Dean from 1824 to 1862.

The fifth window (also by Hardman) is a memorial to the Rev. T. Evans, D.D., a former Headmaster of the Cathedral Grammar School; died 1854.

The sixth window (by Hardman) is in memory of Miss Mary Davies.

The seventh window is a memorial (by Hardman) to Rev. B. S. Claxson, D.D.

The eighth window is a memorial to Rev. John Luxmoore, D.D., who, after being Dean of Gloucester from 1800-1808, was Bishop of Bristol, later of Hereford, and finally of St. Asaph, where he died in 1830.

The ninth window is a memorial to the Ven. Henry Wetherell, B.D., a late Prebendary of Gloucester, who died in 1857.

The tenth and last window in this alley is by Clayton & Bell, and is in memory of Rev. E. Bankes, D.C.L., late Canon of the Cathedral, who died in 1867.

"At the north end of the east alley of the cloister, and almost concealed by the later panelling, is an Early English doorway opening into a vaulted passage or entry, chiefly of the thirteenth century. This entry passes between the east gable of the frater and what I have suggested may have been the common house-garden, and leads straight into the infirmary cloister. The passage is covered by a stone vault of four bays, supported by heavy moulded ribs springing from corbels. The south half of the passage is 6 feet 10 inches wide, but the northern half of the east wall is set back so as to increase the width to 7½ feet. This passage was lighted in the first bay by a single light with trefoiled head, with very wide internal splay. In the wider end were two other openings now blocked. That to the north had a transom two-thirds of the height up, above which the rear-arch is moulded, while below it is plain. The other is not carried above the transom level, and the sill has been cut down and the opening made into a doorway into a house outside; in which state it remained until within the last forty years. That some thirteenth-century building stood here seems evident, and the upper half of the north opening was clearly a window above the roof to light that end of the entry.

"The north end of the entry opens directly into the east alley of the

S. B. Bolas & Co., Photo.]
CLOISTER GARTH FROM THE NORTH-WEST CORNER,
SHOWING THE OLD DRAIN.

infirmary or "farmery" cloister, which is built against the north side of the east end of the frater." (Hope.)

North Alley (east to west).—This "north alley" was closed at both ends by screens, and must therefore have had some special use. From analogy with the arrangements at Durham there can be little doubt that this alley was partly appropriated to the novices. . . . We have curious evidence that the north alley at Gloucester was so appropriated, in the traces of the games they played at in their idle moods. On the stone bench against the wall are scratched a number of diagrams of the forms here represented:

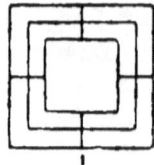 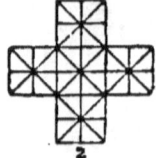 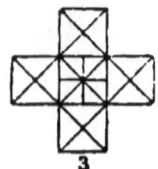

The first is for playing the game called "Nine men's morris," from each player having nine pieces or men. The other two are for playing varietes of the game of "Fox and Geese."

"Traces of such games may generally be found on the bench tables of cloisters where they have not been *restored*, and excellent examples remain at Canterbury, Westminster, Salisbury, and elsewhere. At Gloucester they are almost exclusively confined to the novices' alley, the only others now to be seen in the cloister being an unfinished 'Nine men's morris' board in the south alley, and one or two crossed squares in the west alley." (Hope.)

In the north alley wall some of the lower halves of the five easternmost windows have been re-opened, and the bricks with which they were blocked removed.

The next bay contains traces of a doorway into the cloister-garth that has been blocked.

The **Monks' Lavatory** takes up the next four bays. As Mr Hope says, "it is one of the most perfect of its date that have been preserved. It projects 8 feet into the garth, and is entered from the cloister alley by eight tall arches with glazed traceried openings above. Internally it is 47 feet long and 6½ feet wide, and is lighted by eight two-light windows

THE PRECINCTS AND MONASTIC BUILDINGS 109

towards the garth and by a similar window at each end. One light of the east window has a small square opening below, per-

S. B. Bolas & Co., Photo.]
THE MONKS' LAVATORY.

haps for the admission of the supply pipes, for which there seems to be no other entrance either in the fan vault or the side walls.

Half the width of the lavatory is taken up by a broad, flat ledge or platform against the wall, on which stood a lead cistern or laver, with a row of taps, and in front a hollow trough, originally lined with lead, at which the monks washed their hands and faces. From this the waste water ran away into a recently discovered (1889) tank in the garth." (Hope.)

A plan of this tank is here shown by permission of Mr Waller. It seems to have had a sluice at the west end in order to dam up the water if required in greater volume for flushing the drain.

Opposite the lavatory is a groined almery or recess in which the monks kept their towels. The hooks and indications of doors to this recess are still there. There are traces, too, of screens or partitions in the lavatory arches.

To the west of the lavatory is a "curious arrangement. It consists of a large opening in the lower part of the window, occupying the space of two lights, with a separate chase in the head carried up vertically on the outside. It had a transom at half its height, now broken away, as is also the sill." (Hope.)

It is possible, as suggested by Mr J. W. Clark, F.S.A., that this chase was lined with wood, and was the means by which a bell rope passed out to ring the bell which summoned the monks to meals.

The **North Alley.**—The windows in this alley as far as the Monks' Lavatory have been filled recently, 1896-97, at the expense of Baron de Ferrières of Cheltenham.

There are twenty-seven lights in all, and they constitute the lower part of five windows, a doorway taking the space of three lights. The *eighth* contains a mitre and a crozier, an initial E and the date 1022. This window is an anachronism, as Edric was not a mitred abbot. Abbot Froucester was the first to wear a mitre, in 1381.

Over the lavatory are four windows, also given by Baron de Ferrières. Like the windows in the lavatory, they contain subjects which are in some way connected with water.

The small two-light windows (ten in number) in the Monks' Lavatory have been glazed by Hardman, at the expense of Mr B. Bonnor.

A brass on the wall near the lavatory records that the masonry of the north walk was restored by the Freemasons of the province of Gloucester in 1896.

THE PRECINCTS AND MONASTIC BUILDINGS 111

The **West Alley**.—The north window of three lights has been filled with glass (by Ballantyne) to the memory of members of a Gloucester family named Wilton.

The window was formerly an Early English doorway, which can still be traced. "It retains the upper pair of the iron hooks on which the doors were hung, and was the entrance

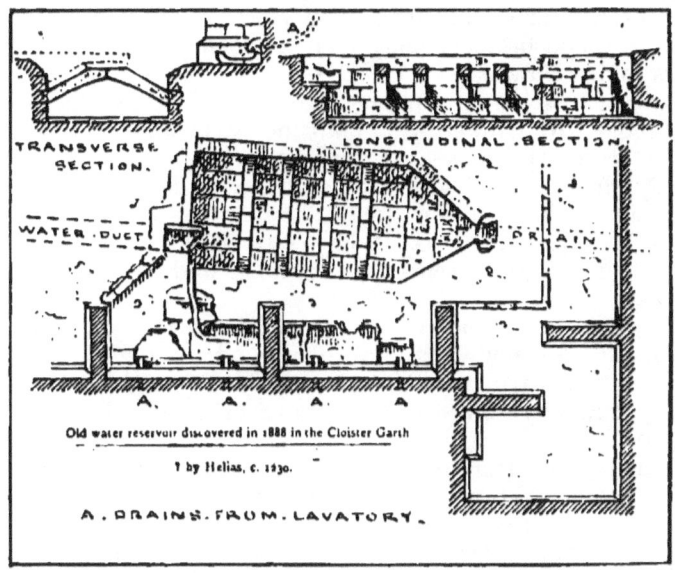

OLD WATER TANK IN THE CLOISTER GARTH.
From a Drawing by F. S. Waller, F.R.I.B.A.

into the great dining-hall of the monks, called the refectorium, or, in English, the frater." (Hope.) The effect of the window is beyond words.

The **Slype**, or covered passage, which is entered from the south-west corner of the cloisters, is a vaulted passage of Norman work, and is under part of the old Abbot's lodging—*i.e.* the present Deanery.

This passage, which is on a lower level than the cloister, was "the main entrance into the cloister from the outer court. This entrance was always kept carefully guarded to prevent intrusion by strangers or unauthorized persons." (Hope.)

The passage served as the outer parlour, in which the monks held conversation with strangers and visitors.

The **South Alley.**—This alley has ten windows each of six lights, but below the transoms the lights are replaced by twenty carrels or recesses, two to each window. This was the place to which the monks resorted daily for study (after they had dined) until evensong. The first window—*i.e.* the westernmost window nearest to the slype—is a memorial to J. Francillon, Esq., a judge of the county court, who died in 1866. The glass is by Hardman.

The first two carrel windows were filled with glass of a simple and inoffensive nature, by T. Fulljames, Esq., and the rest were filled by T. Holt, Esq., to the memory of members of his family, their initials being inserted in the lower corners.

The last window in this south alley is a memorial to R. B. Cooper, Esq., as the brass tablet sets forth. The glass, which is by Hardman, represents the conversion and the execution of St. Paul.

Some of the windows in the cloister are glazed with a peculiarly charming white glass, which admits plenty of light, but is not transparent. The effect is most restful to the eyes after examining some of the bizarre creations in the other windows.

When the cloisters are entirely filled with glass the windows will contain a history of the Life of our Lord.

Britton, in 1828, bemoaned the conversion of the garth into a kitchen garden, and showed how the accumulation of vegetable refuse was injuring the stone-work. There are still residents in Gloucester who can remember Dean Law digging up his own potatoes in the garth. This is now the private garden of the Dean, and is very simply, and therefore charmingly, laid out. It contains the old well of the Abbey.

The present **Deanery** was originally the Abbot's lodging, in which royal persons, high ecclesiastics, and nobles were entertained. When, however, in the fourteenth century, a new Abbot's lodging was built on the site where the episcopal palace now stands, the Abbot's old lodging was assigned to the Prior. The Deanery (which, however, is not shown to visitors), as it now stands, "consists of two main blocks, built on two sides of a court—the one to the south, in the angle formed by the cloister and the church; the other to the west, with the court between it and the cloister." The southern block, which contained the private apartments of the Abbot, consists of three large Norman chambers, one above the other, with their original windows enriched within and without with zig-zag mouldings. Each chamber has also in the north-east corner an inserted or

S. B. Bolas & Co., Photo.]
THE CLOISTER, SHOWING THE CARRELS OF THE MONKS.

altered doorway into a garde-robe tower (shown in Carter's plan, 1807), but now destroyed; and the two lowest chambers have their southern corners crossed by stone arches, moulded or covered with zig-zag ornaments. All these chambers are subdivided by partitions into smaller rooms. Mr Hope says:

H

"The ground storey is entered from a vaulted lobby or antechamber, now modernized and converted into a porch. The first floor has a similar antechamber, as had originally also the second floor, but this has been altered. These antechambers are all of early thirteenth-century date, with a good deal of excellent work remaining about the windows.

"Between the church and the rooms just described is a building of two storeys. The ground storey consists of a vaulted passage, already described as the outer parlour. It is on a lower level than the cloister, which is reached from it by a flight of steps. Over it is a lofty room, also vaulted, which was the abbot's chapel. It is now entered by an awkward skew passage from the first-floor antechamber.

"Both the chapel and outer parlour were once 9 feet longer, but were shortened, and their west ends rebuilt with the old masonry, at the same time that, I have reason to believe, the west front of the church was rebuilt and also curtailed of a bay in the fifteenth century. The first floor of all this part of the house contained the abbot's private apartments, namely, his dining-room, bedroom, solar, and chapel. The second floor was devoted to his own special guests, while the ground storey contained a reception-room, and probably accommodation for one or two servants.

"At the north-west corner of this southern block is a semi-octagonal turret. Until this was altered a few years ago it contained the front entrance into the deanery, and within it a flight of stairs led to a series of landings communicating with the antechambers on the first and second floors, as well as the rooms on the north. Both the turret and the landings replace a much earlier entrance tower, nearly square in form, and of the same date as the antechambers. Many traces of this remain, and show that it was a handsome and important structure.

"The western block of buildings, which is connected with the southern block by the turret and landings, has been so altered in the fifteenth century, and further modernized and enlarged of late years, that it is very difficult to make out the original arrangement. The southern half is two storeys high, with a large hall on the upper floor and the servants' department below. The hall is now divided into two rooms, lined with good Jacobean panelling, and its fifteenth-century roof underdrawn by plaster ceilings.

"At the north end of the hall is another two-storey building. The lower floor is of stone, and now contains various domestic offices. But originally it formed part of a building of considerable architectural importance, as may be seen from the jamb of an elaborate Early English window at the north-west corner. From its position, this Early English building, which seems to have extended westward as far as the inner gate, was most likely the abbot's hall, and here doubtless took place the famous historical dialogue between Edward II. and Abbot Thoky.* Some time before the end of the fifteenth century this hall was cut down, and an upper storey of wood built upon it, of which the east end still remains. At one time it evidently extended further west. Internally it has been gutted, and now contains nothing of interest to show its use."

"The court of the Abbot's house was probably enclosed by covered alleys on the north and west sides to enable the Abbot

* See Hart, i. 44.

to pass into the cloister under cover. In the recent alterations to the Deanery, a block of additional rooms has been built on the west side of the court against the hall." (Hope.)

There is a timber-framed room on the north-west where Richard II. is reputed to have held his parliament. It had a narrow escape some years ago of being destroyed by a fire caused by an overheated flue.

The new lodging for the Abbot (1316-1329, *temp.* Wygmore) was built near the infirmary garden, on the site now occupied by the Bishop's Palace. Drawings of the plans of the old buildings (made in 1856) are in the custody of the Bishop, and reduced reproductions of them are to be found in the "Records of Gloucester Cathedral," 1897, in the article by Mr Hope. Part of the buildings remain on the south side of Pitt Street, and serve to screen the palace from the road.

The **Bishop's Palace** is a modern building, erected in 1857-1862 by Christian on the site of the abbot's lodging.

The so-called **Grove**, laid out by a distinguished headmaster of the King's School, Maurice Wheeler, 1684-1712, on the north side of the church, was used as a school playground till 1855, presumably to the detriment of the windows in the Lady Chapel. It was in that year thrown into the gardens surrounding the east end of the cathedral. These gardens had been originally the monks' cemetery, and adjoining them had been the lay-folks' cemetery, extending along the greater part of the south side.

When all the accumulation of soil was removed, and the ground lowered, the foundations of the old walls were discovered.

The **Cathedral**, or **King's School**, is of Henry VIII. foundation. For many years it was held in the old monastic library. A drawing of it is given in Bonnor's "Perspective Itinerary," 1796. The present buildings date back to 1850.

Photochrom Co. Ltd., Photo.
SOUTH AISLE OF NAVE.

CHAPTER V

ABBOTS AND BISHOPS OF GLOUCESTER

PASSING over the régimes of the Abbesses* and the secular canons, we find that the first Abbot of the Benedictine rule at Gloucester was **Edric** (1022-1028), who in his long rule maintained a very low standard of discipline. His monks seem to have been as much addicted to "ill lyvynge" as the secular canons. He was succeeded by **Wulstan** (1058-1072), a monk of Worcester appointed by Bishop Aldred. In his time Aldred rebuilt the monastery on new foundations. Wulstan died abroad on a pilgrimage to the Holy Land in 1072.

Serlo (1072-1103), the next Abbot, had been the Conqueror's chaplain, and was a man of great strength of character, and of quite a different stamp. He was buried in the abbey church, which he had raised "from meanness and insignificance to a glorious pitch."

Peter, who had been Prior, was Abbot from 1104-1113.

William Godemon, **Godeman**, or **Godemore**, was Abbot from 1113-1130, when he retired.

Walter de Lacy was appointed by Godeman and was consecrated in 1131. In his time, Robert, Duke of Normandy, surnamed Curthose, died at Cardiff after twenty-five years' imprisonment, and was buried in the choir. Walter de Lacy died in 1139, and was succeeded by

Gilbert Foliot (1139-1148), a Cluniac monk, who, owing his position to his relative Milo, Earl of Hereford, was consecrated in 1139. He was made Bishop of Hereford in 1148, and was translated thence to London. Though he owed much to Becket, his patron and tutor, he is said to have taken the king's side in the quarrels with Becket, and to have been instrumental in the latter's assassination.

Hameline or **Hammeline** (1148-1179).

Thomas Carbonel (1179-1205).

* They have been given on pp. 3 and 4.

Henry Blond (or Blunt) (1205-1224). Henry III. was crowned in the Abbey in 1216.
Thomas de Bredon (or Bredone) (1224-1228).
Henry Foliot (or Foleth) was Abbot from 1228-1243.
Walter de St. John died before his installation.
John de Felda (1243-1263).
Reginald de Hamme (or Homme) (1263-1283).
John de Gamages (1284-1306).
John Thokey (or Toky) (1306-1329).
John Wygmore (or Wygemore) (1329-1337).
Adam de Staunton (1337-1351).
Thomas Horton (1357-1377).
John Boyfield (1377-1381).
Walter Froucester (1381-1412).

The succession of Abbots, and the dates of various works executed since Serlo's time, are taken entirely from the particulars in the Chronicles "attributed" to Abbot Froucester (1381-1412), who wrote of the Abbey and of twenty Abbots after the Conquest. These Chronicles are the sole foundation up to that date on which all the histories have been made. There are three copies of them, one in the British Museum, one in Queen's College, Oxford, and one in the Chapter Library, which latter was lost for many years, and ultimately heard of again in 1878 as being in the possession of a bookseller at Berlin, from whom it was rescued on a payment of £150 by the Dean and Chapter.

Hugh Moreton (1412-1420).
John Morwent (or Marewent) (1421-1437).
Reginald Boulers (Boulars or Butler) (Boteler) (1437-1450). He became Bishop of Hereford and was translated to Lichfield in 1453.
Thomas Seabroke (1450-1457).
Richard Hanley (1457-1472). He began to build the Lady Chapel, which was finished by
William Farley (1472-1498).
John Malvern or Mulverne was Abbot for one year (1498-1499), and was succeeded by a monk named
Thomas Braunche (1500-1510), who in turn was succeeded by
John Newton or Browne, D.D. (1510-1514).
William Malverne or Parker (1514-1539).

Parker wrote a Rhythmical History of St. Peter's Abbey, which was reprinted in the appendix of Hearne's "Robert of Gloucester's Chronicle." It was compiled from local records extending up to the time of Abbot Horton.

He subscribed in 1534 to the King's supremacy, and remained Abbot till the dissolution of the greater monasteries. Different traditions are current as to his behaviour. Willis (in "Mitred Abbeys") describes him as losing his pension and the chance of preferment on the score of contumacy. Another tradition asserts that the king promised him the bishopric, but that he died before the appointment was made. The place of his burial is not known, and it is hoped that his tomb will escape desecration for the sake of gratifying mere idle curiosity.

BISHOPS OF GLOUCESTER.

John Wakeman (1541-1549) was the last abbot of Tewkesbury, and chaplain to Henry VIII.

John Hooper (1550-1554) was originally a monk at Cleeve; afterwards became a Lutheran. He could not comply with the statute of the Six Articles, and left Oxford in 1539 and went abroad. In Edward VI.'s reign he preached the reformed doctrine in London. He was instrumental in procuring the deprivation of Bishop Bonner in 1549, and was extremely hostile to Gardiner. He was consecrated Bishop of Gloucester and Worcester by Archbishop Cranmer. He was summoned to London in 1553, and imprisoned. In 1554 his bishopric was declared void. He refused to recant, and was burnt as an obstinate heretic in Gloucester in 1555.

James Brookes (1554-1558). Formerly chaplain or almoner to Bishop Gardiner, and a very zealous Papist. He was delegated by the Pope for the examination and trial of Cranmer, Ridley, and Latimer.

Richard Cheiney or **Cheyney** (1561-1579).

John Bullingham (1581-1598).

Godfrey Goldsborough (1598-1604).

Thomas Ravis (1604-1607), previous to his institution, had been Dean of Christ Church, Oxford. He was one of the translators of the Authorised Version. He was translated to London.

Henry Parry (1607-1610) was translated from Rochester in 1607, and from Gloucester went to Worcester.
Giles Thompson (1611-1612).
Miles Smith (1612-1624). He was one of the translators of the Authorised Version, and is said to have written the preface.
Godfrey Goodman (1624-1640).
William Nicholson (1660-1671).
John Prickett or **Prichard** (1672-1680).
Robert Frampton (1680-1690) was Dean in 1673. He refused to take the oath of allegiance and supremacy after the accession of William III., and was deprived of his office.
Edward Fowler (1691-1714).
Richard Willis (1714-1721) was translated to Salisbury in 1721, and thence to Winchester in 1725.
Joseph Wilcocks (1721-1731). He was translated to Rochester, which see he held, together with the Deanery of Westminster.
Elias Sydall (1731-1733). Translated from St. David's. He was also Dean of Canterbury.
Martin Benson (1734-1752).
William Johnson (1752-1759) was translated to Worcester in 1759.
William Warburton (1759-1779). The well-known editor of Pope's works.
James Yorke (1779-1781). When Dean of Lincoln was appointed Bishop of St. David's, then translated to Gloucester in 1779, and in 1781 from thence to Ely.
Samuel Hallifax (1781-1789). In 1789 he was translated to St. Asaph's, a curious reversal of the usual order of episcopal promotion.
Richard Beadon (1789-1802) was Master of Jesus College, Cambridge, in 1781, but resigned on being made Bishop of Gloucester. Was translated to Bath and Wells in 1802.
G. J. Huntingford (1802-1815). He was translated to Hereford in 1815.
Henry Ryder (1815-1824). Was Dean of Wells, previously Canon of Windsor. He was made Bishop of Gloucester in 1815 and was translated to Lichfield in 1824.
Christopher Bethell (1824-1830). Formerly Dean of

ABBOTS AND BISHOPS OF GLOUCESTER

Chichester. Was Bishop of Exeter for one year, 1830-1831, and was then translated to Bangor.

James Henry Monk (1830-1856). Dean of Peterborough

[H. C. Oakden, Photo.]
MONUMENT TO MRS MORLEY.

in 1822. Consecrated Bishop of Gloucester 1830, and from 1838, when the sees of Gloucester and Bristol were united, was Bishop till his death in 1856.

Charles Baring (1856-1861). Translated to Durham in 1861.

William Thomson (1861-1862). Became Archbishop of York in 1862.

Charles John Ellicott (1863-   ). One of the ablest of modern divines. He was chairman for eleven years of the New Testament Revision Committee. He has published commentaries on various epistles; also works on "Scripture and its Interpretation," "Modern Scepticism"; also a commentary for English Readers on the Old and also on the New Testament.

The sees of Gloucester and Bristol were separated in 1897, and the separation took effect as from January 1st, 1898.

The City.—Gloucester has always been a town of importance, owing to its situation on the banks of the Severn. A Roman camp was formed here in A.D. 43, and later it was fortified with a massive wall (of which the traces still survive), as befitted a military post equal in importance to Circencester, Winchester, Chichester, and Colchester. Much of modern Gloucester rests on Roman foundations.

After the Romans left Britain in 410 A.D., the country suffered from the struggles between its petty kings, and from the invading hosts of the Angles, Jutes, and Saxons. In the end Gloucester, or Gleawan-ceastre, became one of the chief cities of the Mercian kingdom. Alfred held a Witan in the town in 896. Athelstan—the reputed founder of St. John's church—died in it in 940. King Edgar resided there in 965. Hardicanute and Edward the Confessor both held Witans here, but William the Conqueror must always be the central figure in the long line of notable men connected with the history of Gloucester. It was in Gloucester that he spent his Christmas vacations when he could, and it was in the Chapter-House that he took "deep speech" with his wise men, and ordered the compilation of Domesday Book. Rufus, his son and successor, was often at Gloucester, and as Professor Freeman wrote, "in the reign of Rufus almost everything that happened at all, somehow contrived to happen at Gloucester." His death was prophesied by the Abbot of Shrewsbury in a sermon in the Abbey, and warning was sent to the king, but it was of no effect.

Henry I., Henry II., and John were frequently in the town, and the youthful Henry III. was crowned in the Abbey in 1216. Later on he was imprisoned in Gloucester by Sir Simon de Montfort. Edward I. held a Parliament, which passed the celebrated Statutes of Gloucester. Edward II., foully murdered in Berkeley Castle, was buried in the choir of the Abbey.

Richard II., in 1378, held his famous Parliament in the Abbey precincts. In this Parliament the House of Commons secured for itself the right of controlling the financial arrangements of the nation.

Henry IV. and V. assembled their Parliaments in Gloucester, and from Gloucester Richard III. is said to have issued the death-warrant of his nephews. Henry VII. was well received as Earl of Richmond, when he passed through the town on his way to Bosworth Field. Henry VIII., with Anne Boleyn, is said to have spent a week in what is now the Deanery. Later he visited the neighbourhood with Jane Seymour. Elizabeth visited the town, and stayed in the old house next to St. Nicholas' Church. She gave the city the privileges of a seaport, much to the annoyance of Bristol. Gloucester supplied one ship to the navy at the time of the Armada in 1588. In the disastrous Civil War the city played an important part. It is said that the unpopularity of Laud, who had been Dean of Gloucester, led the citizens to side with the Parliament. They held the city under Colonel Massie, against enormous odds, through a long siege, and the king, who had his headquarters at Matson House, was obliged, owing to the approach of Essex with relief, to raise the siege. This was a most serious blow to the failing cause of Charles I.

During the Commonwealth the citizens seem to have lost their heads somewhat, and to have turned against the officer who had saved their city from destruction. Some, too, had made arrangements for demolishing the Cathedral, but fortunately were frustrated in their plans.

As a matter of policy the city congratulated Charles II. at the Restoration in 1660, but without much result, as the walls and gates were ordered to be destroyed. James II. visited Gloucester, and is said to have touched over a hundred persons for the king's evil, a proceeding to which he objected on the score of expense.

The last two Georges visited the city, and Queen Victoria visited it when Princess Victoria, and again later, after her marriage.

The city, like Tewkesbury, is a curious admixture of the

new and the old. It has long emerged from the primitive state, and is now well drained and well supplied with water; but the heavy penalty attaching to transition has been paid, and many old houses and historic buildings, like the Tolsey and others, have disappeared.

The history of Gloucester, commercially, is a history of progress. In Domesday Book, Gloucester is mentioned in connection with iron, the founding of nails for the king's ships. As the ore was obtained locally, this branch of trade flourished till the seventeenth century. Bell-founding was practised as early as 1350 by John Sandre, and one of his bells still hangs and rings in the cathedral tower. Cloth-making, too, was practised, but, declining in the fifteenth century, was superseded by pin-making, for which Gloucester was for many years famous. Glass-making was carried on in the seventeenth century, and the Rudhall family for several generations had a bell-foundry of wide reputation.

Elizabeth made the town a seaport, and it is one still. More than that, it is the most inland port in Britain, owing to the Berkeley Ship Canal, which enables ships to dispense with the awkwardness of a voyage up and down the tortuous and dangerous Severn. It is to this canal that Gloucester owes much of its present trade, as, by sea-going vessels, corn and timber, its staple commodities, are brought in to the many wharves in ever-increasing quantities. To the railways the Great Western and the Midland—the town also owes much of its prosperity, and one great industry, that of railway waggon building, gives employment to many pairs of hands.

In Gloucester, or its neighbourhood, will be found the following buildings of interest:—

Llanthony Priory.—This was formerly an Augustinian convent, with a church attached, founded by Milo, Earl of Hereford, in 1136. It was founded as an asylum for the convenience of the priory in Monmouthshire of the same name, which was so liable to be harried and pillaged by the Welsh. This priory was dissolved in 1539. The church was finally destroyed to make way for the Ship Canal. Some remains exist in a farm, of which the masonry is good. A gateway, in the Perpendicular style, still survives.

St. Oswald's Priory.—In 909 the Princess Elfleda caused the canonised relics of King Oswald to be removed

The Old Judges' House. Westgate St.
Ed Burrow 1894

(From a Drawing by E. J. Burrow.

and richly entombed at Gloucester. She also founded a college for secular priests, but later on it was converted into a priory for regular canons. (Refounded 1153.)

Attached to this priory was a chapel dedicated to St. Catherine, which, after the dissolution of the priory, served for a parish church until its destruction in the siege in 1643. On this site the present Church of St. Catherine was built in 1867-69.

The **Grey Friars** (or College of Friars minor, or Franciscans).—This building formerly stood at the east end of the Church of St. Mary de Crypt.

The **White Friars** (or College of Carmelites).—This building, which was situated without Lower Northgate Street, was founded by Queen Eleanor.

In the time of Elizabeth the college was converted into a house of correction. During the siege in 1643, it was used as a fortress. Portions of it remain incorporated with private houses.

The **Black Friars** (or College of Friars, Preachers).—This college was established by Henry III. in 1237.

Remains of the building are still to be seen on the south side of the thoroughfare called Blackfriars.

The college was dissolved in 1538.

St. Mary de Lode (or St. Mary before the Abbey Gate) stands on the site of a Roman temple. The tower and chancel are all that remain of the original church, the rest being very disappointing, having been built in 1826. The low square tower formerly had a lofty spire, which was destroyed by a storm. The interior of the church has been lately restored. The pulpit is a very fine specimen of carving. In the chancel is a tomb which used to be pointed out as that of Lucius, the first British Christian King.

St. John the Baptist (in Northgate Street).—The original church is supposed to have been founded by King Athelstan.

The present building was built in 1734, the tower being all that is left of the old church. The communion plate was presented in 1659 by Sir Thomas Rich.

St. Mary de Crypt (in Southgate Street) is well worth inspection. It has two crypts—hence its name. The church is Early English, Decorated and Perpendicular, and was built by Robert Chichester, Bishop of Exeter, 1138-1155. It is cruciform in shape, and, though much restored, of great interest.

There are interesting brasses to Luke Garnon, John Cooke and his wife, and a curious squint or hagioscope. In the choir vestry is a monument to R. Raikes. On the north side is a marble monument to Dorothy Snell, by Scheemaker.

The communion plate is all early seventeenth century, and very good, though it has suffered from careless handling.

Close by is the old building of the Crypt Grammar School. The school has migrated to more open quarters.

St. Nicholas is situated at the bottom of Westgate Street, and, owing to alterations in the street, is much below the level of the road. The floor of the church is nearly two feet higher than it was originally. There is much good Norman work, and some good Early English with Perpendicular insertions.

On the south door is a fine (so-called) sanctuary knocker; the door is quite unworthy of the knocker. Under the tower is some good late Jacobean panelling. In the chancel are two squints, four each side, arranged venetian-blind fashion. Several of the tombs are worth inspecting—viz. the Window monument in the chancel, 1659, and one to the wife of Rev. Helpe-Fox, 1657. There is a good tomb to Alderman John Walton and his wife, 1626, which, though in good preservation, is beginning to suffer from damp. There is also a brass, 1585, to Thos. Sancky; and a slab to John Hanbury, who represented Gloucester in Parliament in 1626. A fine view of the cathedral can be got from the top of the tower. The spire was shortened after being damaged in a storm. The chimes are worth hearing.

St. Michael's is situated where the four main streets meet, and near the church was formerly the Cross. The church was restored in 1885, and the monuments and tablets are all grouped together. The most interesting is a brass of 1519, to William Henshawe.

The curfew is still rung from the tower every evening.

Remains of Old Gloucester.—The New Inn was built in Abbot Seabroke's time by John Twynning or Twining (one of the monks), to accommodate the large number of pilgrims who came to the shrine of Edward II.

Close by, at the corner of New Inn Lane, is a beautifully carved angle post and bracket, which has been preserved for many years by being plastered over (*vide* p. 130). The houses on the right-hand side of the lane are also old.

The Gloucestershire Seed Warehouse, 154 Westgate Street, does not look specially interesting, but up the passage, which was formerly "Maverdine Lane," is a portion of the old front of the house. It is a fine specimen of domestic architecture, with very good windows, and has a distinctly Flemish look. There are some good rooms inside, with oak panelling and carving. A chimney-piece bears the text, "I and my house will serve the Lord," and it is dated 1633. The house is usually called the "Old Judge's House," but it is more famous as the house from which Colonel Massie issued his orders in 1643, when Gloucester was besieged by Charles I. (*vide* p. 125).

163 Westgate Street contains a fine panelled room (the greater part dating back from 1530-1550), which was discovered

THE NEW INN.

[From a Drawing by E. J. Burrow.

in 1890 when alterations were being made. It is shown on payment of a fee, which includes a printed description of the house. Some of the carving—such as the Royal Arms of England—seems earlier than 1520, but the arms may have been copied from an earlier document. Near St. Nicholas' Church

CARVING AT NEW INN LANE

is another interesting house, where Queen Elizabeth is said to have stayed in one of her many progresses through the country. The side of the house abuts curiously on the church of St. Nicholas. Inside there is a quaint overmantel, with Elizabethan carving, and E.R. in the centre panel.

In Southgate Street, opposite the Corn Exchange, is a well-known house with a carved front. There is an elaborate

CHURCHES AND REMAINS OF GLOUCESTER

over-mantel dated 1650. It bears the arms of the Yates, the Berkeley, and the Box families. Opposite St. Nicholas' Church is the Bishop Hooper Pharmacy. It is said to be the house where the Bishop was kept closely guarded on the night before his execution.

Remains of the Roman Wall under 36. Westgate St.
E.J. Burrow del /94

The house of Robert Raikes, of Sunday School fame, is a fine house of three gables, and is well preserved.

The house where Raikes held his first Sunday School can still be seen in St. Catherine Street, Hare Lane.

The old Roman wall can be seen in several places—*e.g.* at 36 Westgate Street, at Messrs Lea & Co.'s furniture warehouse in Northgate Street, at Mr John Bellows' in Eastgate Street.

The **Gloucester Candlestick**.—One of the most interesting relics of the Abbey of Gloucester is a candlestick which is now in the museum at South Kensington. It is a remarkably fine piece of metal work, about 16 inches in height, cast by the *cera perduta* process in very pale bronze, richly gilt and decorated. The upright stem is divided into two compartments by bosses, ornamented with the emblems of the Evangelists, and supporting a cup at the top. A triangular base supports the stem, and the whole is enriched with forty-two monsters in various grotesque attitudes, wrestling and struggling with nine human beings.

Round the stem is a ribbon bearing the inscription—

ABBATIS PETRI GREGIS ET DEVOTIO MITIS ME DEDIT ECCLESIE SANCTI PETRI GLOUCESTRE.

Round the cup is a ribbon, on the outside of which a couplet is inscribed—

LUCIS ONUS VIRTUTIS OPUS DOCTRINA REFULGENS PREDICAT UT VICIO NON TENEBRETUR HOMO.

Inside this same ribbon are two hexameters—

HOC CENOMANNENSIS RES ECCLESIE POCIENSIS THOMAS DITAVIT CUM SOL ANNUM RENOVAVIT.

After its removal from Gloucester, the candlestick was given to the Cathedral of Le Mans by Thomas de Poché or de Pocé (POCIENSIS). Subsequently it belonged to the Marquis d'Espaulart of Le Mans, and was sold to Prince Soltykoff for about £800, and finally was bought from his collection for £680 for the Museum at South Kensington.

Bishop Hooper's Memorial stands in the churchyard of St. Mary de Lode, and is on the actual site of the burning. This is perhaps the chief or the only interest in the memorial, as its architectural merit is almost *nil* The inscriptions to prevent defacement are glazed over, and as the glass is broken the effect is wretched. A previous monument to the Bishop was erected at the other end of the churchyard.

An interesting relic of the execution of the Bishop is in possession of the rector of St. Mary's Church—viz. the sergeant's mace, which was the authority of the soldiers who conducted the Bishop down to Gloucester. This mace, which is the only surviving example of a London sergeant's mace, was found in a house in Westgate Street, belonging to a Mr Ingram. It is to be hoped that some day the mace may be deposited in some public national museum.

NOTES, ARCHITECTURAL AND CHRONOLOGICAL

	Style.	Abbot at the Time.	Date.
South Porch, West End of Nave, and Aisles.	P.	Morwent.	1421-1437.
South Aisle of Nave.	Pilasters N., Windows and Groining D.	Serlo. Thokey.	1089-1100. 1307-1329.
Nave.	Piers, Arches, Triforium, Groining E. E., Windows P.	Serlo. Foliot. Morwent.	1089-1100. 1242. 1421-1437.
North Aisle of Nave.	Walls and Groining N., Windows P.	Serlo. Morwent.	1089-1100. 1421-1437.
South Transept.	Tr. (D. to P.)	Wygmore.	c. 1330.
Choir and Presbytery.	P. cased on N. Walls.	Staunton and Horton.	1337-1377.
Ambulatory and Chapels.	Walls and Groining N., Windows D. and P. inserted in N. Openings.	Thokey, Wygmore, Staunton, and Horton.	1307-1377.
Lady Chapel.	P.	Hanley and Fawley.	1457-1499.
North Transept.	P. on N. Walls.	Horton.	1368-1373.
Reliquary.	E. E.	Foliot. (?)	c. 1240.
Cloisters, S.E. part.	D. to P.	Horton.	1351-1377.
,, rest.	P.	Boyfield and Froucester.	1381-1412.
Abbot's Cloister. Chapter-House West-End.	N.	Serlo.	1089-1100.
Chapter-House East End.	N. and P.	Hanley.	c. 1460.
Tower.	P.	Seabroke.	1450-1457.

These Notes are adapted from Mr F. S. Waller's "Notes and Sketches."
N. Norman. E. E. Early English. Tr. Transitional. D. Decorated.
P. Perpendicular.

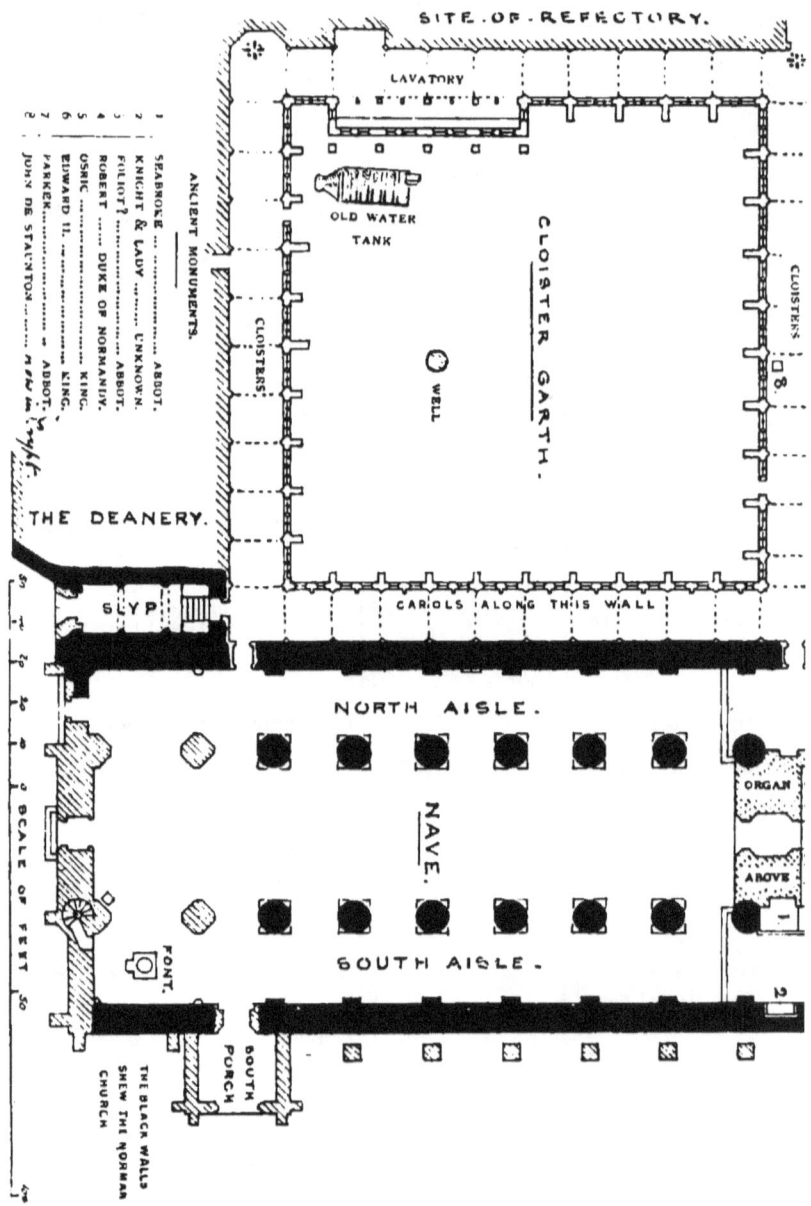

PLAN OF GLOUCESTER CATHEDRAL

GENERAL DIMENSIONS.

	Length. Ft.	Width. Ft.	Height. Ft.
Nave	174	34	68
Aisles	174	15	40
Choir and Presbytery	140	33	86
North Transept	46	34	78
South Transept	46	34	86
Lady Chapel	90	25	46
Chapter-House	72	33	35
Cloisters	147 (±)	12	18½
Tower	40 on roof	40	225
Total length inside	407		
,, ,, outside	425		
Area	30,600 square feet.		

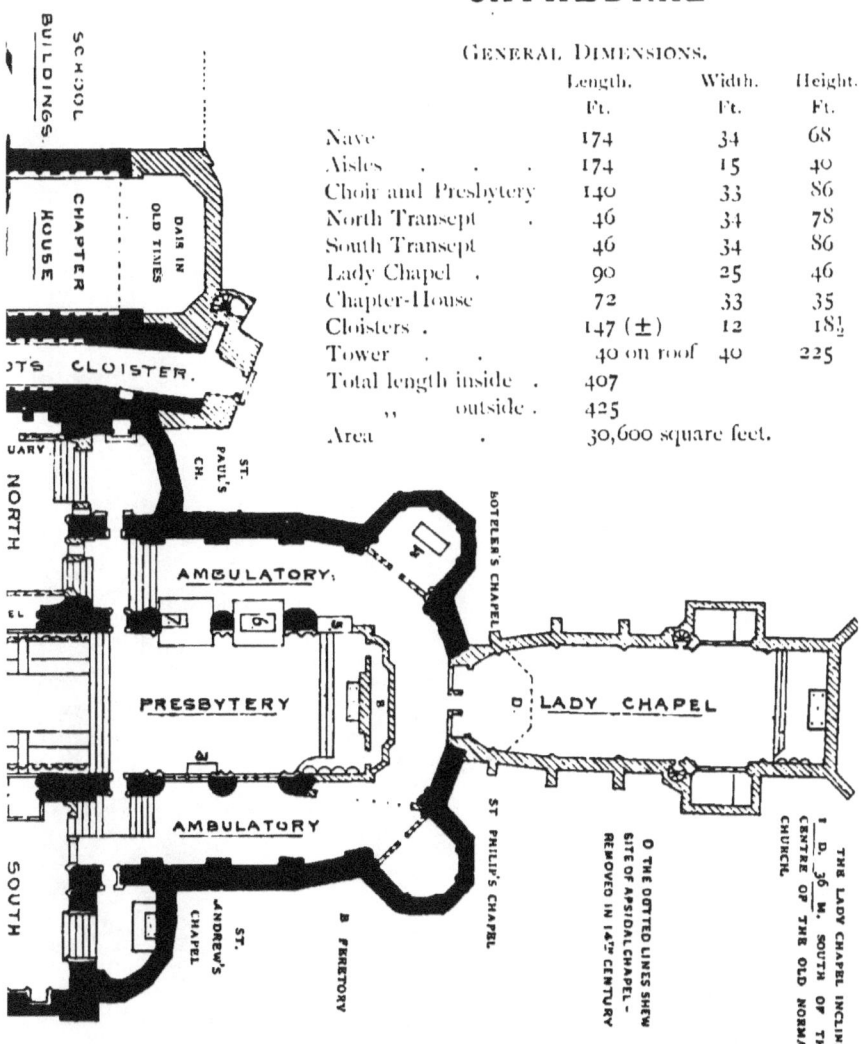

[From a Drawing by F. S. Waller, F.R.I.B.A.

W. H. WHITE AND CO. LTD.
RIVERSIDE PRESS, EDINBURGH

Bell's Cathedral Series.

EDITED BY
GLEESON WHITE AND E. F. STRANGE.

In specially designed cloth cover, crown 8vo, 1s. 6d. each.

Now Ready.

CANTERBURY. By HARTLEY WITHERS. 2nd Edition, revised. 36 Illustrations.
SALISBURY. By GLEESON WHITE. 2nd Edition, revised. 50 Illustrations.
CHESTER. By CHARLES HIATT. 24 Illustrations.
ROCHESTER. By G. H. PALMER, B.A. 38 Illustrations.
OXFORD. By Rev. PERCY DEARMER, M.A. 34 Illustrations.
EXETER. By PERCY ADDLESHAW, B.A. 35 Illustrations.
WINCHESTER. By P. W. SERGEANT. 50 Illustrations.
LICHFIELD. By A. B. CLIFTON. 42 Illustrations.
NORWICH. By C. H. B. QUENNELL. 38 Illustrations.
PETERBOROUGH. By Rev. W. D. SWEETING. 51 Illustrations.
HEREFORD. By A. HUGH FISHER, A.R.E. 34 Illustrations.
LINCOLN. By A. F. KENDRICK, B.A. 46 Illustrations.
WELLS. By Rev. PERCY DEARMER, M.A. 43 Illustrations.
SOUTHWELL. By Rev. ARTHUR DIMOCK, M.A. 37 Illustrations.
GLOUCESTER. By H. J. L. J. MASSÉ, M.A.

In the Press.

DURHAM. By J. E. BYGATE. | YORK. By A. CLUTTON BROCK.

Preparing.

ST. DAVID'S. By PHILIP ROBSON. | CHICHESTER. By H. C. CORLETTE, A.R.I.B.A.
ELY. By T. D. ATKINSON, A.R.I.B.A. | WESTMINSTER. By CHARLES HIATT.
WORCESTER. By E. F. STRANGE. | ST. PAUL'S. By Rev. ARTHUR DIMOCK, M.A.
ST. ALBANS. RIPON.
CARLISLE. By C. K. ELEY. | BRISTOL.

Uniform with above Series, now Ready.

ST. MARTIN'S CHURCH, CANTERBURY. By the Rev. CANON ROUTLEDGE.
BEVERLEY MINSTER. By CHARLES HIATT.

Opinions of the Press.

"For the purpose at which they aim they are admirably done, and there are few visitors to any of our noble shrines who will not enjoy their visit the better for being furnished with one of these delightful books, which can be slipped into the pocket and carried with ease, and is yet distinct and legible. . . . A volume such as that on Canterbury is exactly what we want, and on our next visit we hope to have it with us. It is thoroughly helpful, and the views of the fair city and its noble cathedral are beautiful. Both volumes, moreover, will serve more than a temporary purpose, and are trustworthy as well as delightful."—*Notes and Queries.*

"We have so frequently in these columns urged the want of cheap, well-illustrated, and well-written handbooks to our cathedrals, to take the place of the out-of-date publications of local booksellers, that we are glad to hear that they have been taken in hand by Messrs George Bell & Sons."—*St. James's Gazette.*

"Visitors to the cathedral cities of England must often have felt the need of some work dealing with the history and antiquities of the city itself, and the architecture and associations of the cathedral, more portable than the elaborate monographs which have been devoted to some of them, more scholarly and satisfying than the average local guide-book, and more copious than the section devoted to them in the general guide-book of the county or district. Such a legitimate need the 'Cathedral Series' now being issued by Messrs George Bell & Sons, under the editorship of Mr Gleeson White and Mr E. F. Strange, seems well calculated to supply. The volumes are handy in size, moderate in price, well illustrated, and written in a scholarly spirit. The history of cathedral and city is intelligently set forth and accompanied by a descriptive survey of the building in all its detail. The illustrations are copious and well selected, and the series bids fair to become an indispensable companion to the cathedral tourist in England."—*Times.*

"They are nicely produced in good type, on good paper, and contain numerous illustrations, are well written, and very cheap. We should imagine architects and students of architecture will be sure to buy the series as they appear, for they contain in brief much valuable information."—*British Architect.*

"Half the charm of this little book on Canterbury springs from the writer's recognition of the historical association of so majestic a building with the fortunes, destinies, and habits of the English people. . . . One admirable feature of the book is its artistic illustrations. They are both lavish and satisfactory—even when regarded with critical eyes."—*Speaker.*

"There is likely to be a large demand for these attractive handbooks."—*Globe.*

"Bell's 'Cathedral Series,' so admirably edited, is more than a description of the various English cathedrals. It will be a valuable historical record, and a work of much service also to the architect. The illustrations are well selected, and in many cases not mere bald architectural drawings but reproductions of exquisite stone fancies, touched in their treatment by fancy and guided by art."—*Star.*

"Each of them contains exactly that amount of information which the intelligent visitor, who is not a specialist, will wish to have. The disposition of the various parts is judiciously proportioned, and the style is very readable. The illustrations supply a further important feature; they are both numerous and good. A series which cannot fail to be welcomed by all who are interested in the ecclesiastical buildings of England."—*Glasgow Herald.*

"Those who, either for purposes of professional study or for a cultured recreation, find it expedient to 'do' the English cathedrals will welcome the beginning of Bell's 'Cathedral Series.' This set of books is an attempt to consult, more closely, and in greater detail than the usual guide-books do, the needs of visitors to the cathedral towns. The series cannot but prove markedly successful. In each book a business-like description is given of the fabric of the church to which the volume relates, and an interesting history of the relative diocese. The books are plentifully illustrated, and are thus made attractive as well as instructive. They cannot but prove welcome to all classes of readers interested either in English Church history or in ecclesiastical architecture."—*Scotsman.*

"A set of little books which may be described as very useful, very pretty, and very cheap . . . . and alike in the letterpress, the illustrations, and the remarkably choice binding, they are ideal guides."—*Liverpool Daily Post.*

"They have nothing in common with the almost invariably wretched local guides save portability, and their only competitors in the quality and quantity of their contents are very expensive and mostly rare works, each of a size that suggests a packing-case rather than a coat-pocket. The 'Cathedral Series' are important compilations concerning history, architecture, and biography, and quite popular enough for such as take any sincere interest in their subjects."—*Sketch.*

LONDON: GEORGE BELL AND SONS.

www.ingramcontent.com/pod-product-compliance
Lightning Source LLC
Chambersburg PA
CBHW030356170426
43202CB00010B/1387